EMPIRE OF CAPITAL

EMPIRE OF CAPITAL

ELLEN MEIKSINS WOOD

VERSO

London • New York

For George Comninel,
with thanks for many years of conversation

First published by Verso 2003
© Ellen Meiksins Wood 2003
This paperback edition first published by Verso 2005
© Ellen Meiksins Wood 2005
All rights reserved

1 3 5 7 9 10 8 6 4 2

Verso
UK: 6 Meard Street, London w1f 0eg
USA: 180 Varick Street, New York, ny 10014–4606
www.versobooks.com

Verso is the imprint of New Left Books

ISBN 978-1-84467-518-0

British Library Cataloguing in Publication Data
Wood, Ellen Meiksins
   Empire of capital
   1. Capitalism—History   2. Imperialism   3. Globalization   4. International
   relations   5. Imperialism—History
   I. Title
   330.1'22

ISBN 1844675181

Library of Congress Cataloging-in-Publication Data
A Catalog record for this book is available from the Library of Congress

Typeset by SetSystems Ltd, Saffron Walden, Essex
Printed by R. R. Donnelley & Son, USA

CONTENTS

ACKNOWLEDGEMENTS

I have been exceptionally fortunate over the years in having first-rate post-graduate students, whose own work has inspired me and whose friendship I have continued to enjoy long after they finished their studies. One of them is George Comninel. We have been carrying on a conversation ever since, in 1978, he enrolled in a post-graduate seminar that Neal Wood and I were teaching at York University in Toronto on the Theory and Practice of the State in Historical Perspective, a course that George now teaches at York. I owe him special thanks for his comments on this book and for his always unstinting generosity with his insights and encouragement. So I'm dedicating the book to him.

Another veteran of the state course, Frances Abele, has given me her characteristically lucid and fruitful suggestions on this book, as she has often done before.

Sebastian Budgen at Verso gave me the benefit of his typically critical eye, while Elizabeth Dore and Aijaz Ahmad read one or another chapter on subjects they know much better than I do, to protect me from any egregious gaffes. Thanks, too, to Terry Byres, Peter Gowan and Alfredo Saad-Filho for comments on earlier articles related to this book. I'm also grateful to Tim Clark at Verso both for his copy-editing and for guiding the book through the whole publication process. And, of course, I am, as always, grateful to Neal, for his unflagging support.

The usual disclaimers apply to all of the above, who cannot be held responsible for my mistakes or omissions.

PREFACE TO THE
PAPERBACK EDITION

The first edition of this book went to press before the US had launched its attack on Iraq. But by that time, it had become clear that the preferred policy of the US, in case of a war, would be to follow victory with military occupation. I alluded to this in the book.[1] Yet I believed then, as I do now, that the occupation of Iraq is not intended to establish the US as a colonial empire. If anything, this is confirmed by the mess the US has made of the occupation. US imperialism remains of a different kind, something which I try to explain in this book.

Critics of the Bush administration typically insist that it represents a major rupture in US foreign policy since World War II. There can be no denying the reckless, and even self-defeating, extremism of this regime; but a grand imperial vision has been the essence of US foreign policy since the War. The project of global economic hegemony, supported by massive military supremacy, formally began when the US established its economic hegemony with the Bretton Woods system, and its military supremacy with its atom bombs in Hiroshima and Nagasaki. The Bush administration is undoubtedly more unilateralist and certainly more open about its intention to maintain 'full spectrum dominance', with such massive military superiority that no one, enemy or friend, would think of challenging the US as a global or regional power. But surely global supremacy has been the objective of the US for the past half century.

Some commentators would say that, with the occupation of Iraq, the Bush administration is reverting to an older colonial imperialism, which would indeed be a major departure. But this seems to me to misunderstand the specific nature of US imperialism, then and now, and, indeed, to misunderstand the specificity of capitalist empire.

The United States is the first, and so far the only, capitalist empire. This is so not in the sense that it is the first capitalist power to possess an empire but rather in the sense that it dominates the world largely by manipulating the economic mechanisms of capitalism. The British Empire, which had hoped to exploit the commercial wealth of India without incurring the costs of colonial rule, found itself creating a tribute-extracting military despotism more akin to traditional imperialisms than to a new mode of capitalist hegemony. On the whole, the preference, and the practice, of the US has been to avoid direct colonial rule wherever possible and to rely on economic hegemony, which is less costly, less risky and more profitable.

It is probably safe to assume that the preference of the US is still to maintain economic hegemony without getting bogged down in colonial rule. The occupation of Iraq itself confirms that assumption. It is now painfully obvious that military action was undertaken in the vain hope that the regime could be decapitated, leaving the Iraqi state largely intact but with a more amenable leadership. The imperial power undoubtedly still hopes that it can extricate itself sooner rather than later, establishing its economic hegemony, implanting US capital firmly in the economy and especially in the oil industry, and allowing Iraq to replace Saudi Arabia as a military base, but without an overt colonial presence.

Yet there is a fundamental contradiction here, and that contradiction is a central theme of this book: while the objective of US imperialism is economic hegemony without colonial rule, global capital still – in fact, more than ever – needs a closely regulated and predictable social, political and legal order. We are constantly told – not just by conventional theories of 'globalization' but by fashionable books like Michael Hardt and Antonio Negri's *Empire* – that the nation state is in decline.[2] But imperial hegemony relies now more than ever on an orderly system of many local states, and global economic hegemony depends on keeping control of the many states that maintain the global economy. There is, of course, nothing like the kind of *global* state that could guarantee the necessary order, in the way the nation state has long done for national capital. Nor is such a state remotely conceivable. If anything, the territorial state has become far more, rather than less, essential in organizing economic circuits, through the medium of inter-state relations.

The capitalist mode of economic imperialism is the first imperialism in history that does not depend simply on capturing this or that bit of territory, or dominating this or that subject people. It needs to oversee the whole global system of states and ensure that imperial capital can safely and profitably navigate throughout that global system. It has to deal not just with the problem of 'rogue' states or 'failed' states. It also has to keep subordinate states vulnerable to exploitation. Moreover, to be really effective, it has to establish the military and political supremacy of one power over all others, because, if global capital needs an orderly system of multiple states, it is hard to see how it can tolerate a system in which military power is more or less evenly distributed among various states.

So the first premise of the current US military doctrine, with roots that go back to the end of World War II, is that the US must have such massive military superiority that no other power, enemy or friend, will seek to challenge or equal it as a global or regional hegemon. The object is not simply to deter attack but to pre-empt any rivalry. On the whole, other capitalist powers have accepted this arrangement. It is true that, especially since the disappearance of the Soviet Union, some major allies have not always been entirely compliant. But, given the needs of global capital, it is not surprising that the principal allies of the US – who have also been its principal economic competitors – have generally agreed that the US should have its huge military preponderance and have more or less conceded their own military subordination.

Nevertheless, there remains something to be explained about the behaviour of the United States. It may not be hard to see why global capital in general needs one preponderant military power to maintain an orderly and congenial system of multiple states, but it is not always so clear how the hegemony of the US benefits US capital in particular. We can certainly see why US capital might be interested in some direct imperial interventions like, say, involvement in Latin America. But it is not so easy to find a direct connection between US military supremacy and any specific advantage in global economic competition.

What is easier to demonstrate is that, once this kind of military preponderance exists, it has a dynamic of its own. This is especially true when it has no specific and self-limiting objectives. And what I am arguing here is that, by definition, the new militarism cannot have such objectives, given its wide-ranging and non-specific functions in policing the global state system.

With the kind of unchallenged power it enjoys, we can hardly be surprised that the US will use its huge military preponderance to pursue what any given administration, at any given moment, takes to be its interests, without any constraints – and particularly when its *economic* supremacy is no longer as unchallenged as it used to be. It only takes a George W. Bush to push this use of power beyond all limits. But what I am suggesting here is that military excesses are inscribed in the mission of global capital itself, with or without an extremist administration in the United States.

Since even the massive power of the US cannot by itself embrace the globe, the next best thing is regular displays of military force, if only *pour encourager les autres*. War in Iraq, for instance, was probably not so much a prelude to, say, an invasion of Iran but, on the contrary, an attempt to avoid such a risky venture. Iraq was a suitable target not because it represented a threat to the US and its allies but, on the contrary, because it represented no real threat at all. The US could thus 'shock and awe' the whole region (and the world), with (or so the geniuses in the White House thought) little risk to itself.

The fact that military theatre, or the 'demonstration effect', has become a major element in US military policy makes it hard to predict what will happen next. It was much easier to decipher the pattern of traditional imperialism, when the objectives really were direct colonial rule and territorial expansion. US foreign policy is much more unpredictable because military actions now tend to be detached from any specific objectives. It is often more a matter of asserting dominance than achieving any particular goal.

It must remain a matter of conjecture whether the fiasco in Iraq will cause the US to change course in any significant way. If a primary objective is simply to exhibit the destructive effects of US military power, even this disaster has, in its way, been a success. At any rate, the unseemly spectacle of the US desperately seeking an exit strategy from the debacle without forfeiting its imperial advantage in the region is certainly no guarantee that things will change; and we have, as yet, seen no sign of an alternative to the imperial policy of endless war – not necessarily continuous war but war without end, in purpose or time.

Ellen Meiksins Wood
London, March 2004

PREFACE

As this book goes to press, the world is still waiting to learn whether the US will really launch its threatened war against Iraq. The rhetoric is as bellicose as ever, and the military build-up in the region goes on. It is not, of course, impossible that the Bush administration is hoping for face-saving developments – such as a coup in Iraq or the voluntary departure of Saddam Hussein – that will permit it to extricate itself from an increasingly unpopular and potentially disastrous adventure, and that, contrary to appearances, the White House welcomes the delays occasioned by UN inspections.

But, whatever the outcome of this alarming episode, the explicitly stated policy of the Bush administration invites us to fear the worst, with its emphasis on overwhelming military superiority designed to forestall any possible challenge or rivalry, from friend and foe alike, and its insistence on a unilateral right of 'preemptive defense' against any conceivable, or inconceivable, threat.

Since this Bush Doctrine was clearly announced in September 2002, its liberal critics have typically treated it as a sharp departure from the general trend of US foreign policy since World War II. It is certainly true that an overt commitment to preemptive attack is something different from a policy of containment and, at worst, retaliation, such as the US professed to embrace throughout the Cold War and thereafter; and the inclinations of the Bush regime have no doubt taken US unilateralism to new extremes. It is even possible to argue that the Cheney-Rumsfeld-Wolfowitz-Perle axis represents a distinctively sinister extremism, alien to the mainstream of US politics – to say nothing of the very immediate and personal interest in oil on the part of the administration's principals.

Nor would it be unreasonable to interpret the Bush policy, especially in the Middle East, as approaching the kind of outright colonial empire that the US has generally preferred to avoid, if only because that old form of imperialism has been too risky and expensive, and, indeed, unnecessary for such an overwhelmingly dominant economic and military power. Capitalist imperialism, after all, seeks to impose its economic hegemony without direct political domination wherever it can; and the Bush regime may be closer than its predecessors to violating that practical rule.

But even if we look upon the Bush Doctrine as an anomalous historical detour in the development of US foreign policy, even if we overlook all previous military interventions by the US, even if we ignore the many ways in which earlier administrations have stretched the principles of 'liberal imperialism' to their utmost limits and beyond, the Bush phenomenon cannot be understood except as an extension, however extreme and ultimately self-defeating, of the logic inherent in US foreign policy at least since World War II. And that foreign policy, in turn, makes no sense abstracted from the more general logic of the capitalist system, with its complex and contradictory relations between economic and political/military power.

This book is both a political response to the current situation and an analytic/historical exploration of capitalist imperialism in general, of what drives it and has distinguished it from other imperial forms since its inception. What we are seeing today, as the Bush administration pursues its reckless policies, may be a special kind of madness; but, if so, it is a madness firmly rooted not only in the past half-century of US history but in the systemic logic of capitalism.

Ellen Meiksins Wood
London, January 2003

INTRODUCTION

Anyone who talks about US 'imperialism' is likely to be challenged on the grounds that the US does not directly rule or occupy a single country, anywhere in the world.[1]

And that, indeed, is the difficulty in characterizing the 'new' imperialism. While a few colonial pockets still exist, neither the US nor any other major Western power is today a colonial empire in direct command of vast subject territories. Although the US has a military presence in about 140 countries, it cannot even be said that imperial power unambiguously imposes its rule through the medium of puppet regimes kept in place by imperial military power. Nor, for that matter, is there anything today like the commercial empires that once prevailed because they commanded trade routes by means of superior force or more advanced naval technology.

There was a time when not only colonial rule but economic exploitation of colonies by imperial powers was a fairly transparent business. Anyone observing the Spanish in South America, or, later, the Belgians in the Congo, would have had no difficulty understanding the means by which the wealth of the subject was being transferred to the master. In that respect, traditional imperialism had much in common with certain domestic class relations. Just as there was nothing particularly opaque about the relationship between feudal lords and the peasants whose labour services or rents they appropriated, or between the absolutist state and the peasants whose taxes it extracted, the relationship between colonial masters and their subjects was reasonably clear: the one exerted the force, up to and including genocide, that compelled the others to forfeit their wealth.

In modern capitalism, the class relation between capital and labour is rather more difficult to decipher. Here, there is no direct transfer of surplus labour. The workers pay no rent, no tax or tribute, to their employers. There is no obvious way of distinguishing between what workers keep for themselves and what they forfeit to capital. In fact, far from extracting rent from workers, the employer pays them, in the form of a wage, and that payment appears to cover all the work the worker performs: eight hours' pay, for instance, for eight hours' work. It is not so easy to unravel how the workers create the wealth of capital by means of labour for which they receive no recompense, or, to put it another way, how capital derives more benefit, in the form of profit, from the workers' labour than the workers receive in exchange in the form of a wage. It may be self-evident to any reasonable person that capital accumulation could not take place without a net transfer of surplus labour from workers to capitalists, but how this comes about is far less clear. The Marxist theory of surplus value is a persuasive account of how this transfer takes place, but the fact that such a complex theory is required to explain what ought to be a fairly straightforward transaction testifies to the opacity of the relation between capital and labour.[2] The extraction of rents or taxes from a peasant – where it is obvious that part of what the peasant produces goes to pay landlords or states, whether in kind, labour services or money – needs no such complicated theorization.

More particularly, in the absence of direct coercive force exerted by capital on labour, it is not immediately obvious what would *compel* the worker to forfeit surplus labour. The purely economic coercion that drives workers to sell their labour power for a wage is very different from the direct political or military powers that enabled lords or states in non-capitalist societies to exact rent, tax or tribute from direct producers. To be sure, the propertyless worker has little room for manoeuvre, when selling labour power in exchange for a wage is the only way of gaining access to the means of subsistence, even to the means of labour itself. But that compulsion is *impersonal*; and any coercion that operates here is, or so it appears, imposed not by men but by markets. On the face of it, that still seems a matter of choice, while the only formally acknowledged relationship between capitalists and workers – in sharp contrast, for example, to the juridically recognized relationship of domination and subordination between feudal lord and serf – is an exchange between legally free and equal individuals.

This is not the place to go into the intricacies of value theory or the measurement of the surplus value that represents the exploitation of labour by capital. The point here is simply that, whether or not we acknowledge that what passes between the worker and the capitalist is indeed exploitation, their relationship is not at all transparent, and the means by which, rightly or wrongly, the capitalist appropriates what the labourer produces is by its very nature obscure.

Much the same can be said about the nature of capitalist imperialism, and for much the same reasons. Today, it is harder than it was in earlier colonial empires to detect the transfer of wealth from weaker to stronger nations. But even when it is painfully obvious that such a transfer is taking place, how it is accomplished is no less opaque than the relation between capital and labour, and this opacity leaves a great deal of room for denial. Here, too, there is typically no relationship of direct coercion. Here, too, the compulsions are likely to be 'economic', imposed not (directly) by masters but by markets. Here, too, the only formally recognized relationship is between legally free and equal entities, such as buyers and sellers, lenders and borrowers, or even ostensibly sovereign states.

What makes class domination or imperialism specifically *capitalist* is the predominance of economic, as distinct from direct 'extra-economic' – political, military, judicial – coercion. Yet this certainly does not mean that capitalist imperialism can dispense with extra-economic force. First, capitalism certainly does not rule out more traditional forms of coercive colonization. On the contrary, the history of capitalism is, needless to say, a very long and bloody story of conquest and colonial oppression; and, in any case, the development of economic imperatives powerful enough to replace older forms of direct rule has taken a very long time, coming to fruition only in the twentieth century. But, more particularly, capitalist imperialism even in its most mature form requires extra-economic support. Extra-economic force is clearly essential to the maintenance of economic coercion itself.

The difficulty, again, is that the role of extra-economic force, in capitalist imperialism as in capitalist class domination, is opaque, because in general it operates not by intervening directly in the relation between capital and labour, or between imperial and subordinate states, but more indirectly, by sustaining the system of economic compulsions, the system of property (and propertylessness) and the operation of markets. Even when direct force is applied in the struggle between classes – as when police arrest strikers – the nature of the transaction is likely to be obscured by the ostensible neutrality of the coercive power. Especially in liberal democracies, with universal suffrage and fairly well established civil liberties, the police are not employed by capital but represent a state that, in principle, belongs to all citizens. Today, when powerful states launch military actions against weaker ones, we are given to understand that, here too, force is operating not imperially but neutrally, in the interests of an 'international community'.

To question this is not to say that police action, domestic or international, can never do anything but operate in the interests of a dominant class or imperial power. The point is simply that, in capitalism, even when it does so operate, its purposes are not transparent, as they were when feudal lords exercised their own coercive force against their peasants, or when old imperial states set out explicitly to conquer territory, establish colonies and impose their rule on subject peoples.

To understand the 'new imperialism' – indeed to determine whether it exists at all – requires us to understand the specificities of capitalist power and the nature of the relation between economic and 'extra-economic' force in capitalism. It will be argued in what follows that capitalism is unique in its capacity to detach economic from extra-economic power, and that this, among other things, implies that the economic power of capital can reach far beyond the grasp of any existing, or conceivable, political and military power. At the same time, capital's economic power cannot exist without the support of extra-economic force; and extra-economic force is today, as before, primarily supplied by the state.

The argument here is not that the power of capital in conditions of 'globalization' has escaped the control of the state and made the territorial state increasingly irrelevant. On the contrary, my argument is that the state is more essential than ever to capital, even, or especially, in its global form. The political form of globalization is not a global state but a global system of multiple states, and the new imperialism takes its specific shape from the complex and contradictory relationship between capital's expansive economic power and the more limited reach of the extra-economic force that sustains it.

The conviction that we live in an increasingly stateless world – or, at least, a world in which an increasingly irrelevant state has been subordinated to a new kind of global 'sovereignty' – belongs not only to the mythology of conventional globalization theories. A fashionable book such as Philip Bobbitt's *The Shield of Achilles*, for all its claims that the state as such is not dead, insists that the territorial nation state has been replaced by the 'market state', in essence, a state with no boundaries. This is also the central premise of an ostensibly radical and iconoclastic work like Michael Hardt and Antonio Negri's *Empire*, which argues that the nation state is giving way to a new form of stateless 'sovereignty' that is everywhere and nowhere.[3] The contrasting premise of my book is that such views not only miss something truly essential in today's global order but also leave us powerless to resist the empire of capital.

This book is not a history of imperialism. Although much of its argument will be historical, the purpose of its excursions into the history of empire is to bring into relief the specificity of capitalist imperialism by observing it against the contrasting background of other imperial forms. Some major cases, European and non-European, will not appear at all, or only in passing, such as, among others, the Inca, Portuguese, Ottoman and Mughal empires. The historical chapters will concentrate on a few important examples that were marked by one or another characteristic commonly associated with capitalism – the dominance of private property or the centrality of commerce – in order to highlight the essential ways in which even these cases differ from capitalist empire. Nor does the book claim to be a comprehensive history of capitalist imperialism itself. Here, too, readers will no doubt think of cases that could and perhaps should have been mentioned, or they may object that there is not enough discussion of US imperialism before it matured into its present form. But the main objective of the book is not to present a thorough historical narrative. My purpose is rather to define the essence of capitalist imperialism, the better to understand how it operates today.

In Chapter 1, I shall briefly outline how the economic power of capital has detached itself from extra-economic force, sketching out, in very broad strokes, the relation between economic and political power in capitalism and what implications this has for the relation between the capitalist economy and the territorial state. Chapters 2 and 3 will consider several non-capitalist empires, to exemplify what I call the 'empire of property' (the Roman and Spanish), as against the imperial dominance of a bureaucratic central state (as in China), and the 'empire of commerce' (the Arab Muslim Empire, the Venetian and the Dutch).

The remaining chapters will deal with the development of capitalist imperialism, and the expansion of capitalism's economic imperatives, from the English domination of Ireland to their extension overseas in America, and from the 'second' British Empire in India to today's US-dominated 'globalization'. The final chapter will explore the role of military force in the new imperialism and the contradictions of a system in which a globalized economy is sustained by a system of multiple states – a system in which the extra-economic force of military power is becoming essential to imperialism in wholly new ways, taking new forms in the theory and practice of war.

1

THE DETACHMENT OF ECONOMIC POWER

The new imperialism is what it is because it is a creature of capitalism.[1] Capitalism is a system in which all economic actors – producers and appropriators – depend upon the market for their most basic needs. It is a system in which class relations between producers and appropriators, and specifically the relation between capitalists and wage labourers, are also mediated by the market. This is in sharp contrast to non-capitalist societies, where direct producers typically had non-market access to the means of production, especially land, and therefore were sheltered from the forces of the market, while appropriators relied on superior force to extract surplus labour from direct producers. In capitalism, the market dependence of both appropriators and producers means that they are subject to the imperatives of competition, accumulation and increasing labour productivity; and the whole system, in which competitive production is a fundamental condition of existence, is driven by these imperatives. The effect is, among other things, a distinctive relation between political and economic power, which has consequences both for class relations and imperial expansion.

Economic and Political Power

In non-capitalist class societies, it is not usually difficult to identify the locus of power. Find the source of military and political coercion and you will generally find economic power too. Here, the economic powers of dominant classes depend on 'extra-economic' coercion. Such classes rely on their superior coercive force, on their political and military power and privilege, to extract surplus labour, typically from peasants who, unlike capitalist wage labourers, remain in possession of the means of production, either as owners or as tenants. Capitalism is different, and distinct from all other class societies in this respect. Capitalists – unlike, say, feudal lords – generally need no direct control of coercive military or political force to exploit their workers, because workers are propertyless, with no direct access to the means of production, and must sell their labour-power in exchange for a wage in order to work and to live.

To be sure, capitalists ultimately depend on coercion by the state to underpin their economic powers and their hold on property, to maintain social order and conditions favourable to accumulation. But there is a more or less clear division of labour between the exploitative powers of the capitalist and the coercive powers of the state. In capitalist societies, it is even possible to have universal suffrage without fundamentally endangering capitalist economic power, because that power does not require a monopoly on political rights.

There is even a sense in which only capitalism has a distinct 'economic' sphere at all. This is so both because economic power is separate from political or military force and because it is only in capitalism that 'the market' has a force of its own, which imposes on everyone, capitalists as well as workers, certain impersonal systemic requirements of competition, accumulation and profit-maximization. Because all economic actors depend on the market for everything they need, they must meet its requirements in order to survive, irrespective of their own personal needs and wants.

Capitalism's purely 'economic' modes of exploitation, the growing commodification of life, the regulation of social relations by the impersonal 'laws' of the market, have created an economy formally separate from the political sphere. The other side of the coin is that the political sphere itself exists as a formally separate domain. Although the sovereign territorial state was not created by capitalism, the distincively capitalist separation of the 'economic' and the 'political' has produced a more clearly defined and complete territorial sovereignty than was possible in non-capitalist societies. At the same time, many social functions that once fell within the scope of state administration or communal regulation now belong to the economy. This applies most particularly, of course, to the organization of production and distribution. But, as social life is increasingly regulated by the laws of the economy, its requirements shape every aspect of life, not only the production and circulation of goods and services, but the distribution of resources, the disposition of labour and the organization of time itself.

Coercion in capitalist societies, then, is exercised not only personally and directly by means of superior force but also indirectly and impersonally by the compulsions of the market. The dominant class, with the help of the state, can and certainly does manipulate those compulsions to its own advantage, but it is difficult to trace them to a single source of power.

While capital does require support by state coercion, the power of the state itself is, or so it seems, circumscribed by capital. Many social functions are removed from the sphere of political control or communal deliberation and put under the direct control of capital or made subject to the impersonal laws of the market. On the face of it, although the emergence of an economy also implies a separate political sphere, that sphere seems impoverished, as much of human life is removed from its orbit – which, of course, also means that most aspects of everyday life, those that come within the scope of the economy, fall outside the range of democratic accountability.

One of the most important consequences of this detachment of economic power from direct coercion is that the economic hegemony of capital can extend far beyond the limits of direct political domination. Capitalism is distinctive among all social forms precisely in its capacity to extend its dominion by purely economic means. In fact, capital's drive for relentless self-expansion depends on this unique capacity, which applies not only to class relations between capital and labour but also to relations between imperial and subordinate states.

We have already noted capital's ability to dominate labour by purely economic means and without direct political rule or judicial privilege, in contrast to dominant classes in non-capitalist societies. The economic powers of non-capitalist classes could extend only as far as their extra-economic force, only as far as their political, military, or judicial powers; and, no matter how much surplus was actually produced, accumulation by exploiting classes was limited by what their extra-economic power was able to extract from direct producers. There is an analogous difference between non-capitalist and capitalist imperialisms. Old colonial empires dominated territory and subject peoples by means of 'extra-economic' coercion, by military conquest and often direct political rule. Capitalist imperialism can exercise its rule by economic means, by manipulating the forces of the market, including the weapon of debt.

The state remains vital to this kind of domination, in ways that will be discussed in what follows. But the separation between economic and political domination creates a very complex relation between the state and economic power. This has, among other things, inevitably affected resistance to domination and the conduct of class struggle. The distinctive relation between economic and political spheres within capitalism has always posed a problem for anti-capitalist movements, since the earliest days of socialist opposition. It is, for instance, significant that modern revolutions have occurred not in advanced capitalist societies but in societies where the state has presented a visible target, with a prominent role in direct exploitation. As capitalism develops into its mature industrial form, there tends to be a growing concentration of class struggle in the workplace and a growing separation between 'industrial' and 'political' struggles.

Still, as long as there was some more or less clear connection between national economies and national states, there remained a clear possibility of challenging the power of capital not only in the workplace but at a point of concentration in the state. At the very least, pressure could be put on the state by organized oppositional forces, most particularly the labour movement, to undertake policies that would to some extent ameliorate the worst effects of capitalism. The division of labour between political and economic spheres could even work to the advantage of subordinate classes, and the balance of class forces within the state itself might shift significantly in favour of the working class, so that, even while the state remained within the constraints of the capitalist system, it could act more positively in the interests of workers. There was even a hope that seizure of state power would make possible a more complete social transformation, the replacement of capitalism by socialism.

But today it seems that even the most limited of these possibilities hardly exist. At first glance, the separation of economic from political power seems an even greater, and perhaps insurmountable, problem in today's 'globalized' economy than ever before. Transnational capital seems to have escaped the boundaries of the nation state, the power of capital seems to have become even more diffuse, and the problem of locating and challenging the centre of capitalist power has apparently become even harder. It seems to be everywhere and nowhere.

Yet appearances may be deceptive. A central theme of this book is that the state remains a vital point of concentration of capitalist power, even, or especially, in today's global capitalism, and that the empire of capital depends upon a system of multiple states.

A Declining Nation State?

Let us start from the premise that global capitalism is what it is not only because it is global but, above all, because it is capitalist. The problems we associate with globalization – the social injustices, the growing gap between rich and poor, 'democratic deficits', ecological degradation, and so on – are there not simply because the economy is 'global', or because global corporations are uniquely vicious, or even because they are exceptionally powerful. These problems exist because capitalism, whether national or global, is driven by certain systemic imperatives, the imperatives of competition, profit-maximization and accumulation, which inevitably require putting 'exchange-value' before 'use-value' and profit before people. Even the most benign or 'responsible' corporation cannot escape these compulsions but must follow the laws of the market in order to survive – which inevitably means putting profit above all other considerations, with all its wasteful and destructive consequences. These compulsions also require capital's constant self-expansion. Globalization, however much it has intensified these imperatives, is their result rather than their cause.

These systemic imperatives can certainly operate through the medium of specific transnational corporations, but, as one commentator has put it, 'corporations, as powerful as they are, are only vehicles for capitalists. . . . It's often assumed that corporations are a power in themselves, rather than a particular way in which capitalists organize their wealth.'[2] Any particular organization of capitalist wealth, such as the biotechnology giant, Monsanto, can be challenged, even wrecked. But the capitalists involved can simply restructure their wealth, restore their profits in another form, and resume their destructive activities – all of which Monsanto did, when it entered a merger with another corporation (from which it has since emerged again as a separate company) very soon after one of the most effective anti-globalization campaigns and consumer boycotts seemed to threaten its survival.

If we accept that the problem is not this or that corporation, nor this or that international agency, but the capitalist system itself, we are, of course, left with the problem of tracing capitalist imperatives to an identifiable source. No one can deny that this remains an intractable problem. But, at the very least, we can raise questions about whether the global scope of capital has put it so far beyond the reach of the national state that the state is no longer a major source of capitalist power, a major target of resistance or a potential instrument of opposition. It may be that the opposite is true and that global capital is more dependent on the territorial state than any imperial power has ever been before. We can consider, first, the main functions traditionally performed by the nation state for domestic capital and ask whether these functions have been assumed by transnational organizations acting for 'global' capital.

In every class society, where one class appropriates the surplus labour of another, there are two related but distinct 'moments' of class exploitation: the appropriation of surplus labour and the coercive power that enforces it. In non-capitalist societies, these tended to be more or less united. The separation of economic and political spheres in capitalism has meant that these two moments have been effectively divided between private enterprises (or public enterprises operating on the same principles) and the public power of the state. Of course, any capitalist enterprise has at its disposal an array of disciplinary mechanisms, as well as internal organizational hierarchies, to keep workers in line and at work; and the most effective sanction available to capital is its ability to deny the worker access to the means of labour, that is, its ability to deny the worker a job and a wage, to dismiss workers or to close enterprises altogether. But the ultimate sanction that sustains the system as a whole belongs to the state, which commands the legal authority, the police and the military power necessary to exert direct coercive force.

In capitalism, that coercive power is uniquely separate from the functions of appropriation (even in public enterprises operating on capitalist principles in a capitalist economy). This is in contrast, as we have seen, to the unity of appropriation and coercion in a feudal system, where the lord's coercive power – at bottom, his military power – is also his power to exploit, in much the same way that non-capitalist states have used their coercive power to appropriate surplus labour from direct producers as a means of acquiring private wealth for rulers and officeholders. So, from the beginning, the relation between the capitalist class and the state has been distinctive, with capitalists using their property to exploit propertyless workers, while the state maintains social order at arm's-length from capital.

Capitalism is, by nature, an anarchic system, in which the 'laws' of the market constantly threaten to disrupt the social order. Yet probably more than any other social form, capitalism needs stability and predictability in its social arrangements. The nation state has provided that stability and predictability by supplying an elaborate legal and institutional framework, backed up by coercive force, to sustain the property relations of capitalism, its complex contractual apparatus and its intricate financial transactions.

This has been so since the early days of capitalism. In late medieval and early modern England, there emerged a system of social property relations that increasingly subjected both producers and appropriators to the imperatives of a competitive market. Landlords increasingly sought to subject their tenants to rents determined by market conditions, rather than by custom, and tenants were increasingly obliged to succeed in the market. Both landlords and tenants came to depend on the tenant's enhanced productivity and competitiveness. This was in sharp contrast to non-capitalist conditions, where peasants were sheltered from competitive pressures because they had direct non-market access to land, while lords depended on superior force to extract surpluses from peasants. Markets certainly existed in non-capitalist societies, and peasants often entered them to sell their surpluses and to purchase commodities that they did not produce themselves. But, since neither producers nor appropriators were market-dependent for their access to the most basic means of their survival and reproduction, the market did not act as a 'regulator', nor did it function as an imperative. The effect of English social property relations was to create that kind of market dependence, polarizing the rural population into those who succeeded in competitive conditions, and those who failed to do so and were driven off the land.

This process would hardly have been possible without the support of the state, which, by means of judicial interventions and legislation, helped to make property rights market-dependent. From the beginning, too, intervention by the state has been needed to create and maintain not only the system of property but also the system of propertylessness. State power has, of course, been needed to support the process of expropriation and to protect the exclusiveness of capitalist property. But the state has also been needed to ensure that, once expropriated, those without property in the means of production are available, when required, as labour for capital. Here, a delicate balance has had to be struck. On the one hand, the state must help to keep alive a propertyless population which has no other means of survival when work is unavailable, maintaining a 'reserve army' of workers through the inevitable cyclical declines in the demand for labour. On the other hand, the state must ensure that escape routes are closed and that means of survival other than wage labour for capital are not so readily available as to liberate the propertyless from the compulsion to sell their labour power when they are needed by capital.

This balancing act has been a major function of the state since the earliest days of capitalism, as the history of the English Poor Laws illustrates. In the sixteenth century – in the early years of capitalist development and just at the moment when critics were beginning to cite enclosure as a major social problem – England established the first systematic, national and state-regulated 'welfare' programme in response to the apparent threat to social order arising from the expropriation of direct producers and a growing population of propertyless 'masterless men'. Throughout the subsequent history of the Poor Laws, the need to cope with that problem had always to be weighed against the needs of capitalist employers, culminating in the famous Poor Law Reform of 1834, when Britain's industrial development required a growing and mobile work force. The old system of 'outdoor' poor relief, which had allowed (or obliged) people to depend on support from the parish in which they resided, was now seen as an obstacle to the mobility of labour, which not only kept people tied to their parishes but also removed the incentive to find work in unpopular factories. So 'outdoor' relief was abolished, and poor relief could only be obtained in workhouses designed to be so unpalatable that even work in a factory was more acceptable. There is some doubt about whether the Reform had the desired effect, but there is no doubt about its intentions.

The story of Britain's Poor Laws nicely illustrates how the state has historically intervened to sustain the dependence of labour on capital. Essential to that project has been the indispensable function of the state in controlling the mobility of labour, while preserving capital's freedom of movement. Although the movement of labour across national boundaries has been severely restricted, controlling labour's mobility need not mean keeping workers immobile. It may mean getting them to move to where capital most needs them. The Poor Law Reform of 1834 represents a moment, in the early days of industrial development, when capital needed to uproot labour, to separate it from local attachments. But, while the state has continued to play that role, making labour freely available by movements within and across borders whenever required, such movements have always been rigorously controlled. It has been one of the state's most essential functions to keep a firm grip on the mobility of labour, so that the movements of labour enhance, rather than endanger, capitalist profit. At the same time, the other side of the capitalist relation between political and economic spheres is that it has opened a new terrain of class struggle, and social provision by the state has been substantially modified and enhanced by working-class struggles.

We are constantly told that, today, with the globalization of the capitalist economy, the nation state no longer plays the essential roles that it once did, and that it is increasingly becoming an irrelevance. But no transnational organization has come close to assuming the indispensable functions of the nation state in maintaining the system of property and social order, least of all the function of coercion that underlies all others. No conceivable form of 'global governance' could provide the kind of daily regularity or the conditions of accumulation that capital needs. The world today, in fact, is more than ever a world of nation states. The political form of globalization is, again, not a global state but a global system of multiple local states, structured in a complex relation of domination and subordination.

The first and most basic condition of capitalist expansion beyond the limits of political and military domination is the imposition of economic imperatives, introducing the compulsions of the market where they do not exist and sustaining them where they do. We have seen how the state has operated to achieve this effect in the domestic economy – for instance, by helping to transform the system of property and by controlling the mobility of labour. The imposition of market imperatives has also been the basis of the new imperialism. The economic power of capital may be able to move beyond the reach of military and political power, but it cannot do so unless and until the 'laws' of the capitalist economy are themselves extended – and this is something that needs extra-economic help, both in domestic class relations and in imperial domination. Within the capitalist economy at home, the state has been particularly important in creating and maintaining a class of propertyless workers, who, because they are propertyless, are obliged to enter the market to sell their labour power. On the imperial plane, both metropolitan and local states have played an analogous role in implanting the compulsions of the market.

This does not mean that imperial powers encourage the development of capitalist economies like their own everywhere. It simply means that subordinate economies must be made vulnerable to the dictates of the capitalist market, by forcing them to open their markets to imperial capital and by means of certain social transformations – such as, for example, the transformation of peasants into market-dependent farmers, as subsistence agriculture is replaced by specialization in cash crops for the export market. As farmers become dependent on the market for their very survival, metropolitan powers protect their own domestic agriculture by huge subsidies and import controls; and agricultural producers in subordinate economies are forced to compete with these subsidized farmers, both at home and abroad. Bringing about such social transformations – not simply by direct coercion but, for instance, by means of loans or aid with strict conditions – has been a major function of capitalist imperialism since its inception, and the indispensable instrument has been the nation state.

Older forms of imperialism depended directly on conquest and colonial rule. Capitalism has extended the reach of imperial domination far beyond the capacities of direct political rule or colonial occupation, simply by imposing and manipulating the operations of a capitalist market. Just as capitalist classes need no direct political command over propertyless workers, capitalist empires can rely on economic pressures to exploit subordinate societies. But just as workers had to be made dependent on capital and kept that way, so subordinate economies must be made and kept vulnerable to economic manipulation by capital and the capitalist market – and this can be a very violent process.

On today's morning news, there was a story about an organization of farmers in India who are refusing a British aid programme on the grounds that its conditions would not only force farmers to orient themselves to the export market but, in so doing, would inevitably destroy smaller farmers and concentrate landed property. All too often, imperial states, acting unilaterally or through supranational institutions like the IMF, have succeeded in attaching such conditions to grants or loans designed to restructure the recipient economies to make them more susceptible to economic pressures. Such programmes have had much the same effect, and the same objectives, as analogous state actions in the development of domestic capitalism in Europe – from enclosure to the Poor Law Reform.

The most recent methods of imposing market imperatives are familiar in countries that have undergone 'structural adjustment'. But, in various forms, the process goes back to the earliest days of capitalist imperialism. England, even in the late sixteenth century, was already experimenting with this imperialist strategy, notably in Ireland, as we shall see in Chapter 4. And from the beginning, capitalist imperialism has been affected by one of the main contradictions of capitalism: the need to impose its economic 'laws' as universally as possible, and, at the same time, the need to limit the damaging consequences that this universalization has for capital itself. Capitalism is driven by competition, yet capital must always seek to thwart competition. It must constantly expand its markets and constantly seek profit in new places, yet it typically subverts the expansion of markets by blocking the development of potential competitors (as it did in Ireland, as early as the seventeenth century).

Contradictions

The nation state has been an indispensable instrument in the process of spreading capitalist imperatives, not only in the sense that the military power of European nation states has carried the dominating force of capital to every corner of the world, but also in the sense that nation states have been the conduits of capitalism at the receiving end too. This has been true ever since Britain exposed its major European rivals to the competitive pressures of its own capitalist economy. We shall return to this point in Chapter 6, considering how European states, acting in response to geopolitical and military pressures no less than economic, encouraged capitalist development at home, and how the nation state continues to play an indispensable role in maintaining global capitalism. For the moment, it is enough to emphasize that, for all the globalizing tendencies of capitalism, the world has become more, not less, a world of nation states, not only as a result of national liberation struggles but also under pressure from imperial powers.

These powers have found the nation state the most reliable guarantor of the conditions necessary for accumulation, and the only means by which capital can freely expand beyond the boundaries of direct political domination. As market imperatives have become a means of manipulating local elites, local states have proved to be far more useful transmission belts for capitalist imperatives than were the old colonial agents and settlers who originally carried the capitalist market throughout the world.

But this mode of imperialism, like capitalism itself, has contradictions at its very core. On the one hand, it depends on the separation of the 'economic' and 'political', which makes possible the unbounded expansion of capitalist appropriation by purely economic means and the extension of the capitalist economy far beyond the limits of the nation state. Capitalism has a unique drive for self-expansion. Capital cannot survive without constant accumulation, and its requirements relentlessly drive it to expand its geographic scope beyond national boundaries too. Yet, on the other hand, capital has always needed the support of territorial states; and while the wide-ranging expansion of capitalist appropriation has moved far beyond national borders, the national organization of capitalist economies has remained stubbornly persistent. At the same time, the nation state has remained an indispensable instrument – perhaps the *only* indispensable 'extra-economic' instrument – of global capital. It is possible to imagine changes in existing national boundaries or even in the principal of nationality as we know it. Yet global capitalism without a system of multiple territorial states is all but inconceivable.

At the level of the national economy and nation state, the complex relationship between capitalist appropriation and the coercive extra-economic force it requires to sustain it is relatively straightforward, if fraught with contradictions. There is a more or less clear division of labour: capital appropriates, while the 'neutral' state enforces the system of property, and propertylessness. But the connections become more complicated as capital extends its geographic reach while still depending on more local and territorially limited powers of administration and enforcement. We are just now beginning to learn about the complexities and contradictions of that relationship beyond the borders of the nation state and in the new system of capitalist imperialism.

To sum up: the separation of the economic and the political has made it possible for the economic reach of capital to extend much further than its political grasp – in a way that was never possible for earlier forms of economic exploitation which depended directly on military power and political rule. And yet, capitalism has never been able to dispense with territorial states, with boundaries much narrower than the empire of capital. Capitalist appropriation still requires the support of extra-economic coercion, and a state operating at arm's-length is still required to supply the administrative order and the ultimate coercive force that capital needs but lacks. With a dominant class distinctive in its lack of direct coercive power, capitalism is nonetheless more dependent than any other social form on legal and political order to guarantee the regularity and predictability that capital needs in its daily transactions. Capitalism also depends on extra-economic practices and institutions to compensate for its own disruptive tendencies, for the ravages of the market, and for the propertylessness of the majority on which capitalist power depends.

The trouble is that no form of extra-economic power has yet been devised that can fill these needs apart from the territorial state, which functions on behalf of global capital no less than for local and national. The disconnection between the economic and political moments of capital not only makes it possible for capital to extend its economic reach but also requires it to rely on local states to serve its political needs. On the one hand, the expansion of capital is possible precisely because it can detach itself from extra-economic power in a way that no other social form can; and, on the other hand, that same detachment makes it both possible and necessary for capital's economic hegemony to be supported by territorial states.

As the gap between the economic reach of capital and the extra-economic reach of territorial states grows wider, imperial powers, and the US in particular, have experimented with new forms of extra-economic force to deal with the contradiction. Earlier empires – such as those considered in the next two chapters – had their own weaknesses and instabilities, but this contradiction belongs uniquely to capitalism.

2

THE EMPIRE OF PROPERTY

Today, the military force of the US is by far the most powerful, and the most costly, the world has seen to date. Yet the imperial role of that military power is not at all obvious. When the ancient Romans created their far-reaching Empire – the source of our very language of colonialism and imperialism – they also produced the largest and most expensive military force the world had ever seen. The role of this massive force in the intensive exploitation of the Empire was no mystery. Military power was transparently the essence of Roman imperialism. The transparency of the one case and the opacity of the other tell us a great deal about the differences between capitalist and non-capitalist empires.

China and Rome

The Roman case is significant not only because Western images of empire are self-consciously rooted in it, or even because it was, by the standards of its time, very large and widespread, but also because Rome created and administered its vast empire in a distinctive way, which would thereafter represent the criterion, whether positive or negative, of European imperialism. In a sense, it was the first colonial 'empire', as we have come to understand the word.

Early imperial China, by contrast, had established, already by the third century BC, a very different pattern of rule. This pattern – which, with some variation, formed the framework of Chinese imperial rule for many centuries thereafter – was based on a centralized bureaucratic state, unifying a hitherto fragmented collection of warring states under the rule of the Emperor and administered by a vast apparatus of officeholders. Underlying the coercive powers of the state, needless to say, was military force; but its mission was not colonization of a kind that marked later European empires.

The Chinese imperial state reproduced, on a large scale, a pattern of state-formation that was probably more the rule than the exception in 'high' civilizations of the non-capitalist world: a bureaucratic hierarchy descending from a monarch to administrative districts governed by royal functionaries and fiscal officials, who extracted surplus labour from subject villages of peasant producers for redistribution up the hierarchical chain. Something like this pattern is visible in many of the most highly organized civilizations, from the relatively small and modest states of Bronze Age Greece to the more elaborate and powerful New Kingdom of Egypt, and even, much further afield, the vast empire of the Incas.

The material base of imperial China was the peasantry, which was directly taxed by the state both to sustain its administrative functions and to line the pockets of its officeholders. The imperial state often took measures to block the development of powerful landed classes, even prohibiting the ownership of land by mandarins in the provinces they governed; but office was itself a route to wealth.

This meant that, while peasants lived under oppressive conditions, the imperial state had good reason to preserve the peasantry and its possession of land. It also meant that, while the position of the landed aristocracy fluctuated with the rise and fall of China's successive empires, at the height of China's imperial powers, especially in later centuries, truly great wealth was associated with office. This was less an empire than a single large and over-arching territorial state; and its mode of 'extra-economic' exploitation was less like what we think of as colonial exploitation than like the direct exploitation of peasants by a tax/office state, which in another form existed even in, say, absolutist France.

Like other empires ruled by central bureaucracies, the Chinese imperial state always confronted a dilemma: the direct reach of the central state was necessarily limited, while the means by which that reach could be extended – a proliferation of officers with local administrative and fiscal powers – always threatened to create local power centres and dynasties that might challenge the central imperial power. This tension no doubt limited the state's imperial ambitions.

The Romans were not similarly inhibited. In keeping with its own specific social property relations at home, the Roman Republic, dominated by a self-governing aristocracy of landowners, made a virtue of necessity in its project of imperial expansion, by mobilizing, and even creating, landed aristocracies elsewhere as an instrument of empire from the start. They embarked on a ruthless programme of territorial expansion, a massive land-grabbing operation. The transition from republic to empire certainly required the development of a complex imperial state. But even after the republic was replaced by imperial rule and bureaucracy, the Romans administered their empire with a relatively small central state, through what amounted to a wide-ranging coalition of local landed aristocracies, with the help of Roman colonists and colonial administrators.

If the 'redistributive' kingdom of the ancient world was the foundation of other great non-capitalist empires, the basis of the Roman Empire was a very different social and political form. The ancient Greek and Roman states were 'city-states' governed not by monarchies or bureaucracies but by self-governing communities of citizens, with varying degrees of inclusiveness. The state apparatus was minimal, and the governing bodies were assemblies of one kind or another, with relatively few standing offices. Although peasants as well as landlords were citizens in, for instance, both Athens and Rome, the balance of relations between rich and poor, large landowners and peasants, varied and was reflected in different political dispensations, such as the democracy in Athens or the aristocratic republic in Rome. But in all cases, land, not state office, was the principal source of wealth; and taxation was never the problem for Greek and Roman peasant-citizens that it has been for other peasants throughout history. At the same time, the peasants' relative freedom from dependence, protected even in aristocratic Rome by their civic status as citizens of the city-state, encouraged the development of slavery as an alternative source of surplus labour for larger landowners.

The city-state or *polis* became the basis of the Hellenistic empire, which created a new kind of imperial hierarchy. Here, although there was a monarchical centre, the hierarchy descended from the monarch to the *city*, dominated by a local aristocracy of private landholders, who often had land grants from the monarch. The Romans essentially took over this form of imperial rule, adopting its 'municipal' structure. Although in the East the Empire tended to be superimposed on already well developed political and economic institutions, the western parts of the Empire were reshaped by this 'municipal' form of organization. But while the *polis* in ancient Athens had been remarkable for its democracy, the Romans, in keeping with their aristocratic base at home, used the municipal form (even in rural areas with no real urban centre) to organize and strengthen local aristocracies. In fact, where no sufficiently dominant propertied class existed, the Romans were likely to create one; and everywhere they encouraged the development of Romanized local propertied elites.

The material base of the Empire was correspondingly distinctive. The growth of slavery certainly marked out the Roman Empire from other great empires. But, although slavery became very important in the imperial homeland, it never dominated the Empire as a whole; and throughout Rome's imperial history, peasants probably still remained the majority of the population outside Rome itself. There is certainly a sense in which the peasantry was no less the basis of the Roman empire than it was of the Chinese imperial state, but peasants played a very different role in Rome than they did in China.

In many parts of the Empire, local peasantries continued to play their traditional role as producers of surplus labour for landlord and state, by means of rent and tax, especially in those regions in the eastern Empire and North Africa where the Romans largely took over already well developed political and economic structures. But the Roman peasant himself was a different story. He was the military backbone of Rome's imperial expansion. Many peasants experienced exploitation more as soldiers than as rent-producers or taxpayers, and their creation of the empire was the principal means by which they enriched their aristocratic compatriots. Their military role, and their long absences on military campaigns, also made them vulnerable to expropriation at home, which certainly encouraged the concentration of land and the replacement of peasants by slaves to work the large estates. The proposition that the Empire rested on the peasantry must then be amended to take account of the fact that, in the process of imperial expansion, the army was increasingly professionalized, as soldier was increasingly detached from peasant.

The revenues of empire no doubt helped to keep Roman peasants relatively free from the burden of taxation, at least for a time. Imperial expansion also provided an alternative income and even allowed them, up to a point, to replace their ancestral lands with new colonial possessions. As for their replacement by slaves, 'one of the main functions of slavery', as a distinguished historian of Rome has put it, 'was that it allowed the elite to increase the discrepancy between rich and poor without alienating the free citizen peasantry from their willingness to fight in wars for the further expansion of the empire.' Nevertheless, the fact remains that 'Roman peasant soldiers were fighting for their own displacement.'[1]

The Roman propertied classes were vastly enriched by this whole process, from expropriation of peasants at home, appropriation of great wealth from imperial revenues and, above all, from land. It may seem strange to say so, but the Roman 'elite' was arguably more dependent on the acquisition of land than any other ruling class had ever been before. In other 'high' civilizations, the possession of extra-economic power through the medium of the state had been a primary means of appropriation, even where private property existed and commerce was very well developed.

In China, even during the last imperial dynasty, when private property was well advanced and trade conducted on a very large scale, the Manchu conquerors (who ruled China until 1912) derived their wealth less from appropriating land than from seizing hold of the bureaucracy and its apparatus of office and tax. Truly great wealth in the empire derived from office rather than property, and the imperial state had an interest in obstructing the growth of the landed aristocracy, while preserving peasant possession as a source of taxation. By contrast, the Roman aristocracy, at home and abroad, was above all a class of landowners. There have been societies in which wealth derived from land has been an avenue to lucrative public office – such as absolutist France or even the highly commercialized Dutch Republic. For the Romans, conversely, office was an avenue to land. Even as imperial administrators, they were primarily interested in looting local populations (officially or unofficially) largely for the purpose of investing the profits of office in land. While this preoccupation with land did not prevent the Roman aristocracy from engaging in large-scale commercial enterprises, land was nevertheless its only secure and steady source of wealth. That fact alone goes a long way toward explaining their ruthless imperialism and militarism.

The Empire of Private Property

Unlike other imperial states whose overbearing power tended to impede the development of private property, the Roman Empire consolidated the rule of property as an alternative locus of power apart from the state. This combination of imperial state and strong private property was reflected in the Roman law, which produced both a distinctive conception of absolute individual property (*dominium*) – very different from the loose conceptions of possession characteristic, for example, of the ancient Greeks – and also something approaching a notion of sovereignty (*imperium*) – a public right of command attached to civil magistrates and then the emperor – which distinguished Roman ideas of the state from the Greek idea of the *polis* as simply the community of citizens. While the conceptions of *dominium* and *imperium* had roots in the Republic, they developed in tandem and came to fruition in the administration of the Empire by means of the alliance between property and state.

This mode of imperial administration did not, of course, preclude the need for military force. On the contrary, the Empire was a military construction above all else, and the word *imperator* applied to great military commanders before it designated emperors. If anything, the Empire's dependence on private property made it even more reliant on military power, in the form of a huge standing army. The presence of Roman legions throughout the Empire was a necessary bulwark of local administration, a substitute, in a sense, for a top-heavy centralized state at home in Rome.

The Roman Empire, then, rested on a dual foundation: a strong system of private property and a powerful military force. This proposition may seem self-evident, even banal. But, just as it cannot be taken for granted, even in societies with well developed private property, that the greatest wealth necessarily derives from it, we cannot assume that imperial expansion is always an extension of appropriation by that means. More commonly, before the advent of European imperialism, extending the reach of imperial rule meant, above all, extending direct appropriation by the state. Just as states and dominant classes at home derived great wealth from taxation, so, too, did imperial domination extend that mode of appropriation, through the medium of tribute and tax.

The Roman case represents a significant departure from this pattern, but not because it ceased to depend on imperial taxation – which it certainly did not. It is even possible to say that the Romans, like others, exploited their Empire largely by means of taxation (especially since taxes at home were more limited). But taxation here was a medium for other modes of appropriation, more than a means of direct exploitation itself. Private land, and the wealth derived from it, were the essence of the imperial exercise; and even the Roman mode of administration, while forging bonds of Empire by granting various privileges and even offices to imperial subjects, depended above all on strengthening the rule of private property in the hands of local elites, as well as colonial settlers and administrators.

Maintaining the army was the primary cost of the Empire, and this in turn affected the use of land, as a direct source of supplies or as the basis of taxation. Yet the logic of this empire derived not from tax-hungry officeholders but from a land-hungry aristocracy of private property. The reliance on colonists and local propertied classes certainly allowed the Empire to reach far beyond the grasp of its central state administration (in a way that, for instance, the Chinese imperial state did not), but it also created its own problems of enforcement. The Empire relied on such a huge standing army precisely because its defining purpose was the private acquisition of land, and because, in the absence of a vast state apparatus, the Empire depended on a fragmented coalition of local aristocracies, whose own powers were grounded in their private property, in a dangerously disjointed polity policed by widely dispersed Roman legions.

The fragmentation and particularism of the Empire also placed a premium on cultural ties and on universalistic ideologies that could help bind the fragments together. The network of communication and the remarkable system of roads which enabled military and commercial movements also served as conduits of Roman culture. The Roman citizenship, which was extended beyond Rome to the Empire, was geographically and ethnically inclusive in its conception, quite unlike, for example, the exclusive Athenian idea. Athenian citizenship, at least in principle, designated active political agency in a direct democracy, and was therefore resistant to very wide extension. The Roman citizenship – perhaps because it had always been, even in the Republican period, associated with aristocratic dominance over a majority of lesser citizens – was more adaptable to spatial expansion and extension to local elites, who were allies, as much as subjects, of their Roman rulers. Active republican citizenship increasingly gave way to a more passive legal identity, which had more honorary or symbolic value than political force.

The Roman law, as it developed to encompass the Empire, was also conceived in universalistic terms, first in the form of the *ius gentium*, which was meant to apply to all peoples, as distinct from the *ius civile*, specific to Roman citizens, until the citizenship spread and rendered the distinction irrelevant. The Roman law countered (up to a point) the particularisms of local laws and customs; and its principles were essential to the Roman definition of property, which spread throughout the Empire. But its dominance depended upon its willing acceptance and implementation by Romanized local elites. Both Roman law and Roman citizenship played a major part in unifying the Empire, but they did so by creating an ideological at least as much as a political or administrative unity.

It would also be hard to explain the spread of Christianity if Roman imperial functionaries – including, finally, the Emperor Constantine who 'Christianized' the Empire – had not recognized the utility of the 'universal' religion, the first of its kind, as an instrument of imperial order. The very idea of a 'universal' church, as distinct from the traditional local or tribal cults, which included Jewish monotheism, would probably not have emerged if the Roman Empire itself had not been conceived as 'universal', claiming to represent a universal human community.

In order to play that imperial role, the Christian religion had to undergo a significant transformation. It had to be transformed from a radical Jewish sect, which opposed the temporal authority of the Empire, into a doctrine amenable to, and even encouraging, imperial obedience. That transformation can be traced from St Paul to St Augustine, both of them Romanized imperial subjects – one a citizen of Rome in its imperial ascendancy, the other as Bishop of Hippo who witnessed the imperial decline – and two of the most ingenious ideologues any empire has ever produced. In their hands, Christianity became not a politically rebellious sect of a tribal religion but a 'universal' spiritual doctrine that sought salvation in another world and 'rendered unto Caesar' his unchallenged temporal authority.

The pattern of imperial decline very clearly reveals the logic of the Empire. The mode of administration, and the system of private property on which it was based, meant that the Empire tended toward fragmentation from the start; and in the end, that tendency prevailed. The imperial bureaucracy grew, above all for the purpose of extracting more taxes – as always, largely to maintain the Empire's military power. But the growth of the bureaucracy was a sign of weakness, not of strength. With no significant new conquests after the first century AD, the Roman army was over-stretched in keeping control of the existing empire, while the burdensome bureaucracy and the tax-hungry state grew in order to sustain the army. The burden this imposed on Rome's imperial subjects simply hastened the decline. The so-called 'barbarian' invasions were less a cause than an effect of Rome's disintegration. By the time these incursions became a fatal threat and not just an annoyance, a crumbling state had long since become an intolerable burden to peasants and a dispensable nuisance to landlords.

It is a striking fact that the so-called 'fall' of the Empire took place in the West and not in the imperial East, where the pattern of rule was more like that of other ancient empires: a bureaucratic state in which land remained largely subordinate to office. It was in the western empire, where state rule was diluted and fragmented by aristocracies based on huge landed estates, that the weaknesses of the Empire proved fatal.

As the imperial state imploded, it left behind a network of personal dependence binding peasants to landlord and land – a development encouraged by the state itself when, in a time of crisis, it tied many peasants to the land, no doubt for fiscal purposes. A new form of dependent peasantry, the colonate, in which tied peasants and freed slaves merged, came to replace the old forms of chattel slavery. In the centuries following the 'decline and fall', there would be various attempts to recentralize this fragmented system under one or another dynastic monarchy, with successive cycles of centralization and repeated fragmentation, as one or the other element in the uneasy Roman fusion of political sovereignty and landed property prevailed. But the fragmentation of the Roman Empire is still recognizable in European feudalism, a system of parcellized power based on property, with political and economic power united in a feudal lordship dominating and exploiting a dependent peasantry without the support of a strong central state.

From Rome to Spanish America

The fragmentation of the Roman Empire may have been the cause of its demise; but, while it lasted, that same fragmentation, with its base in private property rather than an overwhelming bureaucratic state and wealth derived from office, allowed the Empire, with the support of a farflung army, to extend its reach far beyond the territory that such a state could have governed directly. Conquest and colonization of widely dispersed territories would continue to be the pattern of later European empires. This also meant the continuing combination of relatively strong property (descended from Rome via feudalism) with strong but relatively small central states.[2]

This is not to say that post-feudal European states, notably Spain, failed to develop bureaucracies at home, and sometimes even in the colonies, to govern their domestic territories, their growing empires on the European continent and their very distant colonies. The point is rather that property, especially in land, at home and abroad, was never overtaken by state appropriation as the basis of ruling-class wealth, and that no such vast and distant colonies could have been administered at all without dependence on local powers grounded in property. The primary mode of imperial expansion was not absorption of new territory into a single bureaucratic apparatus but rather the dispersal of political and economic power bound up with private property, governed by an imperial state from a very great distance.

Spain, while building a centralized monarchy at home and an extended empire in Europe, would create the largest overseas empire the world had ever seen. It did so by means of precisely such a public/private partnership. Its medieval reconquest of European lands from the Moors, and its spread into Africa and the Canaries, provided a model for further expansion. This was a model based less on the great bureaucratic kingdoms of the past than on feudal parcellization. It is certainly true that Spanish monarchs, especially Ferdinand and Isabella, sought to protect their own royal powers and to prevent the emergence of a hereditary feudal aristocracy in the colonies; and they created a state bureaucracy unlike anything that had hitherto been seen in Europe. But they presided over Spain's massive imperial expansion into the Americas by farming out the tasks of empire to private conquerors in pursuit of private wealth.

The contractual agreements between the Spanish Crown and the *conquistadores* in America had their roots in similar agreements with leaders of military expeditions against the Moors. Although settlement of the Americas would inevitably create its own distinctive patterns of development, the original model was clearly the kind of exchange between monarch and military leaders familiar to European feudalism, in which conditional rights of property and jurisdiction had been vested in the lord in exchange for military services. The essentially private conquerors of America were granted various rights to land and the fruits of conquest in the form of booty and human captives. This did not create a feudal aristocracy in the European sense, since the monarchy sought in various ways to prevent such a development, recognizing the Indians as owners of the land they had cultivated at the time of conquest, while the Spanish State claimed the rest, together with all the sub-soil. But the tension between the royal state and the colonial elites would never cease to haunt the monarchy.

The colonial settlements that occupied America also followed the medieval model of the *Reconquista*. Just as conquerors had done in lands recaptured from the Moors, the *conquistadores* established towns, incorporated by the Spanish Crown, as the main centres of settlement, reproducing the urban institutions of medieval Castile. Surrounding themselves with their supporters established in municipal offices, the conquerors governed the adjacent countryside, in which land was worked by conquered indigenous peoples.

There emerged a variation on the *encomienda* system, which had already existed in recaptured Moorish lands. Settlers were granted effective control of tributary labour, ostensibly in exchange for their provision of religious education and military protection to the people under their control. In theory, the *encomienda* was not a grant of land, since the Indians were recognized as owners of the land, though nearby plantations might belong to the *encomandero* and be worked by the same Indians. Nor was the *encomandero* entrusted with political jurisdiction over them. But in practice, these restrictions had little effect on the settlers' control over their subjects or on the harshness of the system. It became a murderously extreme form of exploitation, little short of slavery and responsible for killing huge numbers of Indians. So destructive was this system that it eventually gave way, under pressure from both state and Church, and also, no doubt, because it was ultimately self-defeating. But it was replaced by other hardly less oppressive forms of exploitation, including the system of peonage that would survive into the twentieth century.

The empire became, more than anything else, a quest for gold and silver. Although the conquest was certainly genocidal, its military toll vastly increased by disease, the Spanish seem to have had more to gain from conquering and ruling the indigenous peoples than from completely exterminating them, requiring a labour force more than they needed empty territory, in mines as well as agricultural plantations. The civilizations they encountered were extremely diverse, ranging from nomadic hunter-gatherers to densely populated, socially stratified and technologically complex empires. While the conquest destroyed these empires, the conquerors certainly had much to gain from their technologies, their agricultural skills and their experience of large-scale public projects.[3]

This mode of imperial expansion created its own ideological needs. It is true that the conquest, even the overthrow of powerful indigenous empires, was achieved by surprisingly small military forces; and the Spanish military presence in the colonies was never very large. But there was no mistaking this empire as anything other than an empire of conquest; and the Spanish, unlike other European empires after them, were unambiguously explicit that what they were justifying was indeed conquest. Christianity played the primary role in justifying the empire. It is certainly true that Christian theology also produced trenchant critiques of imperial expansion and raised far-reaching questions about the legitimacy of conquest and war. But it is testimony to the remarkable flexibility of this moral discourse that a theology critical of the Spanish empire in the Americas could be mobilized no less in its defence.[4]

Early justifications of the empire, especially at a time when the Spanish sovereign was also Holy Roman Emperor, presented it as something like a mission on behalf of the Christian world order, based on donation from the pope in the form of papal Bulls. In this respect, it followed in the tradition of the true Roman Empire and its claims to be acting on behalf of a universal world order. But the difficult relationship between the Spanish monarchy and the papacy made appeals to papal donation an awkward defence. To make matters worse, the available theological arguments against the claims of the papacy, which worked in favour of the monarchy, tended also to argue against the Spanish conquest. Theologians of the Salamanca School argued that the pope, though he was the spiritual leader of Christendom, had no temporal authority over the world, nor did the pope have authority of any kind over non-Christians. This meant not only that there was no such thing as a universal temporal empire but also that Spain could not rely on papal donation and claim legitimacy for its conquest on the grounds that it was bringing Christianity to infidels, or even that it was punishing savages for violations of natural law.

These arguments, whether they were motivated by humanitarian revulsion at imperial atrocities or simply defending the monarchy against the papacy, challenged the right to impose Spanish domination on the Americas. Yet a justification of empire emerged from the very same theological tradition. Having accepted that the old arguments based on the universal temporal authority of the church and the papacy would not serve, the new justification relied instead on the 'just war'. Colonialism might not be justified on the grounds of papal authority, but there were various legitimate reasons for waging war – to defend the 'innocent' or, much more broadly, to promote the values of 'civilized' (i.e. European) life. Just as a republic could go to war in self-defence, war could be waged on behalf of a universal 'human republic' (the Roman theme again) threatened by behaviour that violated its particular standards of peace and good order. Any conquest resulting from a just war could establish legitimate domination. The principle of war in self-defence could thus embrace anything including universal conquest, not to mention slavery.

While this ideology of conquest drew on Christian justification, it was still clearly rooted in the military values of a feudal aristocracy and feudal conceptions of glory, something very different from the peaceful virtues of commerce and agriculture that would be claimed for the (no less bloody) English, and to some extent French, imperial ventures. But the Spanish Crown also invoked Christian doctrine in its attempts to control the feudal ambitions of colonial settlers and to prevent the emergence of a hereditary aristocracy in America. The restrictions imposed by the monarchy on the growth of slavery and on the *encomienda* system may have been in part genuinely motivated by ethical and religious concerns, but there can be little doubt that the effort to curtail the independent power of the settlers was an overriding consideration.

To some extent, the Spanish monarchy succeeded, controlling the colonists, with the help of the state bureaucracy at home and, up to a point, by means of local administrations which it implanted in the colonies to counteract the power of the settlers. In Peru, for instance, an elaborate state bureaucracy was created, in large part for the purpose of regulating forced labour in the mines. But, while a hereditary feudal aristocracy never did evolve in the Americas, it was clearly impossible for the Spanish state to govern its colonial territories without permitting local landed classes their continued domination of the land and its people. The Crown was even compelled to relinquish its hold on what became by far the most important colonial export – gold and silver from South American mines. Having begun by claiming the mines discovered on royal land as part of the royal patrimony, the monarchy found it impossible to exploit this source of huge wealth on its own and ended by giving up the mines or leasing them out in exchange for a share of the yield.

The empire nonetheless became essential to the wealth of Spain at home, increasingly dependent on bullion imported from the colonies instead of on domestic agriculture and industry. That dependence has often been blamed for the decline of the Spanish economy from the seventeenth century onward. Spain's empire, in Europe and abroad, became a burden rather than an economic asset, not least in its demand for taxes. But, while such reasons can be cited for the relatively rapid and dramatic decline of what, for a time, had been the greatest imperial power the world had yet seen, we must consider, too, the inherent instability of any world empire that depends on extra-economic powers but can extend the geographic reach of those powers only by diffusing them. The rebellion of local colonial ruling classes and the wars of colonial independence that were to follow testify less to the emergence of a revolutionary bourgeoisie than to the legacy of the uneasy colonial balance between imperial state and local power based on landed property.

Spain, like Rome before it, was able to extend its imperial domain by vesting power in local landed classes; and it was able to profit hugely from the empire for a time. In that sense, the economic reach of the imperial state already exceeded its political grasp. Yet the essential dependence on extra-economic force – from the military conquest on which the whole system rested to the various forms of extra-economic exploitation adopted by the conquerors, to say nothing of Spain's major role in developing the European slave trade – meant that the economic hold of the empire was always limited by the capacities of its extra-economic power. It would be a very long time before purely economic imperatives would extend the reach of empire further than this.

3

THE EMPIRE OF COMMERCE

Between the Spanish Empire and today's economic imperialism of 'globalization', economic imperatives have undergone a long history of development, first in England and eventually throughout the world. In the meantime, even the most advanced kind of industrial economy has not precluded much more direct forms of extra-economic colonial exploitation, such as the notoriously brutal colonization of the Congo in the nineteenth century by King Leopold II of Belgium. At a time when the Belgian economy was one of the most industrialized in the world, Leopold appropriated the territory as a personal fiefdom and embarked on a genocidally ruthless extraction of the region's wealth. The British Empire may have been the first to mobilize economic imperatives as an instrument of imperialism, perhaps as early as the late sixteenth century; but it, too, as we shall see in the next chapter, would even much later establish more direct colonial rule over a territorial empire, especially in India. It was not until the twentieth century that economic imperialism became strong enough to dispense with older, extra-economic forms of colonial rule.

Yet there had existed for a very long time empires whose primary objective was not appropriation of territory, settlement or resource extraction, but dominance in international trade. To be sure, every major empire depended on trade, and all of them were, to a greater or lesser exent, constructed to enhance control of trade. Both the Chinese and Roman empires, for instance, commanded trade on a massive scale; and the Spanish Empire, too – though perhaps less a maritime commercial power than its Iberian neighbour, Portugal, and more interested in extracting gold and silver from the Americas than in controlling trade routes – was heavily involved in trade and clearly not indifferent to the commercial benefits of its colonial possessions (to say nothing of its role in the growing slave trade). But some empires were commercial in their very essence, more dedicated to the control of trade than territory or even forced labour. To say that they were commercial empires, however, is not to say that their imperial domination was based on the kinds of economic compulsion we associate with capitalism. Here, too, extra-economic power was the basic operating principle.

The Arab Muslim Empire

There have been various kinds of commercial imperialism. It would not be entirely unreasonable, for instance, to describe the ancient Athenian empire, such as it was, as rooted in trade – though any such description requires much caution and qualification. Contrary to a tendency among some historians in the past to exaggerate the commercial character of the Athenian democracy, it was not a mercantile city like the commercial centres of medieval Europe. Nor did Athens ever create anything like the territorial empire of the Romans. If nothing else, the dominant social property relations and political organization of democratic Athens precluded the exploitation of peasants as soldiers in the Roman manner. While the Athenian army could certainly be called a peasant army, peasants remained peasants, rooted in the land, and the army's movements were limited by the agricultural cycle. The democracy also helped to preserve the status of the peasant-citizen at home, and typically maintained its imperial 'alliances' by installing democratic constitutions in subordinate cities, keeping local aristocracies in check. Athenian imperial ambitions, then, were not clearly determined either by the demands of a landed aristocracy or by mercantile interests.

At the same time, a kind of imperial expansion did become a means of ensuring the food supply, by compensating for domestic agricultural deficiencies; and the military actions of the Athenians were largely directed toward that end. They increasingly depended on their navy to maintain control of sea routes for the purpose of importing grain; and this meant huge expenses – for instance, for building and maintaining ships – which in turn required more imperial revenue to sustain them, in the form of tribute from dependent 'allies'.

In that sense, it would be more accurate to say that the empire grew in order to sustain the navy, rather than that the navy grew in order to effect imperial expansion. While the Athenians built their naval force, and the imperial domination that sustained it, to supplement their food supply, this was hardly a commercial empire based on an overwhelming control of lucrative trade, largely for the benefit of merchant classes, their patrons, and the states or trading companies that sustained them. That kind of empire did, however, exist elsewhere, and would be a major force in the following centuries, notably in the Islamic world and then in Europe.

The Arab Muslim empire and late medieval or early modern European commercial empires like the Venetian or the Dutch diverged in many ways, but they had one fundamental thing in common. However much their respective states differed, they all sustained their domination over a wide geographic expanse not simply by means of extending the reach of a single powerful state but by perfecting their role as vital economic links among separate markets in dispersed communities and regions. If the cohesion of the Chinese imperial state depended on its bureaucratic apparatus, and territorial empires like the Roman were held together by a network of landed aristocracies, the connecting threads in the commercial empires were supplied, above all, by merchants and traders. But while such commercial links were, to some extent, a substitute for the political cohesion supplied by a single overarching state, they were no less dependent than other empires on military force – if not to capture territory (though these empires did that too, sometimes on a very large scale) then to guarantee control of trade routes, by land or sea, or to force other states, even other empires, to accept their trading posts, merchant settlements, trade concessions and often monopolies.

The Arab Muslim Empire was certainly created by conquest, which covered a huge area, from Asia to Spain. By military means, the Arabs gained control of trade routes, together with the vast and prosperous territories that depended on them: already existing commercial cities, the states that governed them and the agricultural lands whose peasants had long produced state revenues, as they would continue to do. The Arabs spread out from the Arabian heartland in all directions, to North Africa and Spain, to Sicily, the Mediterranean coasts of Europe, to Anatolia, the Balkans and India. But, while the conquered lands were, at first, held together by a network of armed camps, or camp-cities, and then by a succession of bureaucratic states with the usual array of officers, it was the underlying networks of trade that laid the foundations both for this military expansion and for the spread of Islam. The early conquests built on already existing commercial connections, while the later expansion of Islam into Central Asia, southeast Asia, China and sub-Saharan Africa depended as much on trade as on military success.

In the pre-Islamic age, the Arabs had already enjoyed a strategic position along the major trade routes; but, with the Muslim conquests, the nature of Arab trade as well as its extent were transformed. Instead of simply trading goods in local markets or relaying them from one strictly local merchant to the next along a long-distance trade route, the Muslim Arabs created a system of wide-ranging direct trade, especially in spices, without intermediaries and with merchants reaching far beyond their local markets, taking charge of conveyance across great distances. Islam followed along the same routes.

The networks of commerce and religion were the unifying threads of a fundamentally fragmented empire. The differences and divisions among regions, cities, and tribal communities, and then the dynastic conflicts that divided the Islamic world into competing branches of the Muslim religion, to say nothing of geographic and ecological obstacles, from mountains to deserts, did prevent the long-term stability of any single ruling state apparatus. The original empire won by the conquests of Muhammad and his successors gave way not only to a series of competing dynasties and fragmented territories but eventually to several distinct state power centres, and the loss of conquered territories, especially those they had gained in Europe. Yet, though the tendency to political fragmentation was there from the beginning, the social and economic cohesion of the Arab Muslim world was able to reach beyond the power of any particular state.

That cohesion was based on an elaborate economic network,

joining a chain of huge cities and widely dispersed regions by major trading links. Those links, in turn, were underpinned by a structure of laws and offices. But this was not simply the structure of a single, vast territorial state. It was the unique religious formation associated with Muhammad and his followers. Muhammad himself, born around 570 in Mecca, an important commercial city, belonged to the tribe of Quraysh, the ruling tribe of his city and noted, even in the Koran, as merchants. He married into a trading family and managed his wife's commercial affairs. The critical moment in the development of Islam, Muhammad's move from Mecca to become a religious leader in Yathrib (later Medina), apparently took place at the instigation of merchants in Yathrib, who had commercial links with Mecca. Islam established a comprehensive system of laws and moral norms that supplied a common regulatory order, together with a common culture, that Muslim merchants and craftsmen carried with them across a very wide and diverse territory.

The Muslim religion seems to have been both a condition for and a consequence of the Arab network of trade. In the centuries after the foundation of Islam, the religion and its hierarchy developed as a means of organizing trade relations, even in the absence of effective political unity. Presiding over this network of cities was a body of religious leaders, the *'ulama* (or *ulema*), who were not only preachers but also teachers and judges, and whose higher ranks, together with merchants and master craftsmen, constituted the urban elite, in wealth as in other respects. Although state administrators were also based in the cities, the markets and religious establishments were the dominant physical presence, far more visible than the centres of government.

The detailed and stringent regulations laid down by Islamic law, *sharia*, on matters ranging from marriage and inheritance to commercial contracts and profit, were, perhaps in their intention but certainly in their effect, a condition of the social and economic links that bound the Arab Muslim world together. While Islam was not, as its critics often like to claim, spread simply by conquest, and while they did not impose their religion on all their conquered territories, religious links were vital to maintaining the commercial empire. Even when that empire was superseded by regional states, much of its social and economic cohesion remained. This fragmented political order, joined by commercial and religious ties, lasted until the Ottoman Empire superimposed upon it yet another overarching bureaucratic state, which nonetheless gained much of its own power from the persistence of old networks, commercial and religious.

The Muslim Empire, then, was at its very heart a commercial formation, based on a network of trade centres which formed the largest cities in the world outside East Asia, such as Cairo and Baghdad, bound together by merchants, craftsmen and religious figures. This pattern of development brought with it a remarkable cultural flowering and developments in scientific and mathematical knowledge that would profoundly influence the European world.

The cities were surrounded by rural populations of landowners, peasants and pastoralists of various kinds. In the Middle East and North Africa alone, there had long been a wide spectrum of rural production, ranging from the cultivation of olives in coastal regions or grain production in river valleys and plains, where livestock could also be raised, to deserts where date-palms were grown and camels were bred by means of long-distance seasonal migration. When the Arabs conquered Spain in the early eighth century, they brought with them not only various crops hitherto unknown in Spain but also agricultural techniques and irrigation systems, bringing cultivation to previously barren regions.

So the empire was rooted in the land, and the Arab rulers depended on the wealth created by rural producers, maintaining earlier systems of taxation and the agricultural production on which they were based. But the countryside, especially as the empire evolved, was subordinated to the city, which exercised its control by appropriating rural surpluses to sustain the urban population, military forces and the state bureaucracy. There is a striking contrast between this world and medieval Europe, whose history, despite the emergence of great towns and the growth of trade, is dominated by a landed aristocracy. The most notable exception to this medieval European rule was the Italian city-states (to which we shall return), which themselves formed commercial empires radiating out from cities that dominated their surrounding countryside.

In the Arab Muslim world, even state dynasties with their origin and base in the countryside ruled through this network of cities. 'In order to survive,' writes a major historian of the Arab world, 'a dynasty needed to strike roots in the city: it needed the wealth to be derived from trade and industry, and the legitimacy which only the *'ulama* could confer. The process of formation of dynasties consisted in the conquest of cities. A conqueror would move up a chain of cities lying on a trade-route.'[1] While the presence of a powerful ruler, who might even be able to divert trade routes to benefit his capital city, enhanced the growth of a town, the extension of his rule typically depended on the underlying urban networks of religion and commerce.

It should now be possible to identify some of the ways in which a commercial empire such as this, despite – or perhaps precisely because – of the centrality of towns and trade, was not governed by the economic imperatives associated with capitalism.

Capitalist imperatives, as we saw in Chapter 1, derive from the market dependence of all economic actors. Both appropriating and producing classes must enter the market to obtain the most basic conditions of their self-reproduction, and the relation between them is also market-dependent. The first question is whether any such market dependence existed in this – and other – commercial empires.

Direct producers in the Muslim Empire were still predominantly rural. Although the Arabs engaged in a significant slave trade (with slaves typically supplied, as early as the eighth century, by the Venetians), which was used to supply not only domestic service in the cities but sometimes also agricultural labour in areas such as the upper Nile valley and in Saharan oases, the rural work force in the Muslim Empire consisted predominantly of peasants and pastoralists. These generally produced the bulk of their own subsistence, though they might go to market to sell surpluses, with the proceeds of which they could buy other goods. Their subsistence was in that sense not market-dependent. More fundamentally, their access to land, the basic means of production, was not dependent on the market or success in competitive production.

Rural producers were, however, subject not only to exploitation by landowners, typically as sharecroppers, but, even more so, to the superior force of their rulers in the city; and it was by this means, above all, that they were exploited. The principal instrument was taxation; and, while urban dwellers also paid taxes, state revenues probably always had a predominantly rural source. Underlying the power of taxation was, of course, the military force of the rulers; but it also worked to the advantage of other members of the urban elite, particularly those to whom the state farmed out the collection of taxes, so they had effective control over rural producers as a source of personal wealth. There were also religious establishments that imposed their own obligations. In other words, producers were not driven to produce, nor were appropriators enabled to appropriate, by the forces of the market. The operative principle was the extra-economic power of extraction, exercised by appropriators with superior authority and coercive force at their command.

Urban producers, the craftsmen who congregated in the major centres of trade, may have depended on local markets for foodstuffs (though even this observation must be qualified, since they could often rely on their own gardens to supply at least some of their own food); but they, too, were sheltered from market imperatives. Their access to the means of production was not mediated by the market. Craft skills and shops were typically passed down from father to son and governed by tradition, rather than by the laws of competitive markets. While their own products did go to market, this was not the kind of market in which success was determined by price competition and labour productivity. It was a network of exchange in which the skills of craftsmanship, or perhaps long-standing personal connections, were the basis of successful business. A business of this kind typically went on for many generations without any change in production or increase in size.

Although some master craftsmen did belong to the urban elite, craftsmen selling their own products in local markets rarely acquired great wealth. It was merchants engaged in conveyance and carrying trade over great distances who benefitted most from this commercial system. Even trade by merchants who conveyed domestically produced goods to other markets increasingly gave way to more lucrative transport of goods from elsewhere, such as China, India or Western Europe. In that sense, commerce became more, not less, detached from production; and the great merchants were likely to be those engaged, typically through agents, in long-distance trade in valuable commodities and luxury goods produced elsewhere.

But whether the merchant stayed within the Arab world and traded in domestic products, or operated a transit trade in goods produced far away, the principle of trade was essentially the same: the age-old practice of commercial profit-taking, buying cheap and selling dear. That kind of profit – as distinct from the production of surplus value in capitalism – depended not on superiority in competitive production but on various extra-economic advantages, such as political power or religious authority – which allowed the imposition of unfavourable terms of exchange on producers – or widespread mercantile networks and command of trade routes, guaranteed by military power. This form of commercial gain is in direct opposition to capitalist profit. Specifically capitalist profit is generated by greater labour productivity and cost-effectiveness, in a market sufficiently integrated to impose certain common conditions of competitive production. Non-capitalist commercial profit, by contrast, depended on the separation of markets, buying cheap in one and selling dear in another; and truly great mercantile wealth derived from advantages in negotiating separate markets that were distant from each other, with the help of military power.

The Venetian Empire

Italy has been called the 'weak link' of European feudalism, because seigneurialism was weaker there than elsewhere in Europe and because the dominance of landed aristocracies was, especially in the northern city-states, overtaken by the rule of urban classes, who dominated the surrounding countryside. But if these city-states departed from the feudal pattern, they nevertheless played a critical role in the larger feudal system, as a commercial link within that fragmented order and as a means of access to the world outside Europe.[2] It can, of course, be said that even this role depended on the dominance of landed classes in the feudal system as a whole. It was, above all, the wealth of landed aristocracies, and the monarchies that emerged from them, that drove feudal commerce, especially in the quest for luxury goods and for the materials of warfare on which their economic power depended. But the great Italian trading centres were able to profit from that wealth in the way they did because they existed within the feudal network while remaining in some ways outside it.

The distinctive position of Italian city-states in the European economy may be rooted in certain more or less unbroken continuities with the Roman Empire. Older Roman landholding patterns persisted, with a larger proportion of free peasants, as distinct from serfs. The relatively strong position of the towns perhaps also owed something to the Roman municipal system, in which towns were the social and political domain of Romanized local elites, who effectively governed the surrounding countryside. But, while the imperial elites had been overwhelmingly landed classes, a new kind of urban ruling class emerged in medieval Italy.

Cities like Florence and Venice became what have been called collective lordships, dominating the *contado*, the surrounding countryside, and extracting wealth from it in one way or another, not least to sustain the public offices that, directly or indirectly, enriched many members of the urban elite – in a pattern reminiscent of other tax/office states we have encountered. In this respect, they were unambiguously non-capitalist in their mode of exploitation, depending on the coercive power of the city to appropriate surplus labour directly, not only for the purpose of maintaining civic revenues but also for the benefit of urban elites who owed their power and wealth to their civic status. But, while rural production was needed to provide the city with supplies and revenues, the real wealth of these city-states and their dominant classes was generated by commerce and financial services. Exploitation of the countryside was more a means than an end, a service to the urban economy. The question is whether the logic of that economy was capitalist, or whether the commercial system itself still followed a non-capitalist logic.

Florence and Venice certainly traded in commodities produced in their own cities, such as Florentine textiles or Venetian silk and glass; and the ruling urban classes certainly encouraged and exploited not only commerce but production, with merchants organizing and investing in production as long as market opportunities were attractive enough. But, while production in these city-states was substantial, the circulation of goods and the provision of financial services were the sources of great commercial wealth. Trade was conducted on non-capitalist principles, depending not on cost-effective production and enhanced labour-productivity in a market driven by price competition, but rather on extra-economic advantages, such as monopoly privileges, with the aid of especially sophisticated commercial and financial practices (double-entry book-keeping for instance, is supposed to have originated in Florence). In some cases, where these city-states imposed their military force on colonies, they could exploit forced labour in the production of marketable commodities – as the Venetians did, for instance, by funding the use of slaves for sugar production in Crete and Cyprus. But Venetian gains from slavery derived not only from the republic's own exploitation of slaves but from its central role in the early slave trade, supplying slaves to the Arab Caliphate already in the eighth century. In any case, while Italian merchants could and did benefit from the extra-economic exploitation of producers, at home and elsewhere, the most militant commercial interests were engaged in speculation, not production.[3]

This is not to say that production could not or did not adapt to changing conditions and market opportunities. But the ultimate secret of success in these commercial city-states was their command of trading networks. This, in turn, depended not only on the quality of the products they produced but also on the extra-economic advantages that gave them superiority in controlling and negotiating markets or conveying goods between them, both their own domestic goods and particularly those produced elsewhere. Political power in the city was at the same time economic power; and in external trade, which was by far the most lucrative commercial activity, military force remained the basic condition of commercial success.

The urban elite was likely to respond to inadequate commercial opportunities not by enhancing labour productivity and improving cost-effectiveness but by squeezing producers harder by means of extra-economic coercion. They might, in fact, find it more profitable to withdraw from production altogether, and even from trade. In Florence, for instance, the greatest commercial families, notably the Medici, moved into more lucrative non-productive enterprises, such as financial services for monarchs and popes, and, indeed, public office, up to and including dynastic rule of the city-state. Even for those who remained in trade, appropriation of great wealth still depended on civic powers and privileges, on their status in the city and on the extra-economic power of the city-state itself.

At bottom, then, the commercial success of these city-states was based on military force. Economic competition in these non-capitalist economies was less a matter of price competition than rivalry among merchants, commercial cities or states over direct control of markets. The city-states of northern Italy were constantly at war with their neighbouring rivals, to maintain control of the *contado* as well as dominance in trade; and local wars among Italian cities occurred with the normality and regularity of football fixtures. In the process, both Florence and Venice for a time established control not only over their own *contado* but over neighbouring cities and their surrounding countryside.

A major feature of these commercial societies was the commercialization of war (the Italian *condottiere* was, after all, the model mercenary soldier). But nowhere was the connection between commerce and war more symbiotically close than in the construction of Venice's commercial empire. The city's location gave it privileged access to trade between East and West, but to preserve its commanding position required control of eastern Mediterranean sea routes. This naturally brought Venice into regular military conflict with rivals, to say nothing of pirates. Maintaining its commercial expansion also required control over rivers and mountain passes on the Italian mainland, which was a strong motivation to establish a territorial empire on Italian soil and beyond.

The Venetians turned military force not only into a means of directly policing their commercial dominance but into an exchangeable commodity in its own right. From the beginning, the city-state's commercial success depended on expanding its reach beyond Italy, and that demanded not only military force and a vastly superior navy but commercial ingenuity, particularly the exploitation of war as a commercial resource. In the early days, for instance, Venetian commercial expansion relied on trade concessions from the Byzantine Empire, which granted Venice commercial privileges and rights to trading posts in exchange for military aid.

By far the most notorious example of their commercialization of war occurred during the Fourth Crusade, in the early thirteenth century. Having been asked to transport Frankish Crusaders to Palestine by ship, the Venetians characteristically exacted a very high price. When the final payment was not forthcoming, they simply changed the terms of the bargain, agreeing to ship the armies in exchange for a military diversion: before continuing on their way to their objective, the Crusaders would stop to quell rebellion in Venice's Dalmatian port colonies, which was endangering the Republic's lucrative Adriatic trade routes. Then, for good measure, the Venetians had the crusading armies attack their rival in Constantinople and depose the Greek Orthodox emperor. This attack on a

Christian centre may seem an odd undertaking for the Crusaders (who never did make it to the Holy Land), but it was certainly profitable, as they looted the great city in the infamous sack of Constantinople. As for the Venetians, with the fall of the Byzantine emperor their imperial expansion now embraced a substantial portion of the old Roman Empire.

Venice did not maintain its rule on the Italian mainland and beyond by means of a large and centralized bureaucratic state, but the old Roman method of reliance on local oligarchies could not quite serve its purpose either. Although the Roman Empire had controlled important networks of trade through its command of major commercial links, notably Egypt, trade had been a means to an end, not the imperial end in itself. The Empire was dominated by a landed aristocracy whose principal objective was land, and it was not so troubled by commercial rivalries. For Venice, the object of the imperial exercise was not so much to capture territory for its own sake as to dominate trade, and commercial dominance was not an easily divisible commodity. In a non-capitalist market, where trade was not driven by price competition and competitive production but depended on direct extra-economic command of markets and success in extra-economic – particularly military – rivalry, commerce was more of a zero-sum game, where one city's gain was another's loss. This meant that rival cities and their mercantile elites had to be defeated or at least weakened.

At home, Venetians continued to be governed essentially by an urban oligarchy (even under the ostensible rule of the Doge). But in its conquered Italian territories its typical mode of administration was, like that of the Florentine territorial state, to grant a degree of autonomy to subject cities, with the constant threat of Venetian intervention, while undermining local oligarchies by keeping control of the *contado* and enhancing its powers and privileges, as a counterweight to the urban elites. The result was that, when subject cities rebelled, the *contadini* were inclined to turn against their local oligarchies in favour of Venetian rule. In its non-Italian dependencies, Venice adopted various other stratagems. In parts of Greece, for instance, it dotted the landscape with fortresses, so that, in case of resistance to their rule, the Venetians could buy time while their overwhelming naval power was mobilized. In the great prize of Constantinople, the Venetians put in place a weak foreign figurehead who presented no challenge to Venice's commercial supremacy.

In all these cases, the dominant feature of Venetian imperial rule was the symbiosis of commerce and war. This pattern defies a host of conventional assumptions in European culture (despite a long and bloody history of wars over trade) about the association of commerce with peaceful enterprise, as against the military values of feudalism. The inseparability of commerce and war, of economic and extra-economic power, also flies in the face of conventions about the connection between commerce, the city and capitalism. What is perhaps most striking about a commercial empire like Venice, and other Italian commercial city-states, is the combination of a supremely commercial economy and extra-economic means of appropriation under a highly militarized urban rule: in a sense, an urban and commercial feudalism.

It is no doubt significant that the greatest Italian political thinker of the Renaissance, the Florentine Niccolò Machiavelli, is the one who most closely identifies the civic virtues of the republican citizen with the military virtues of the Roman soldier. Commercial values are nowhere visible in his political works, and commercial activity barely figures at all. If anything, he shows contempt for the quest after wealth; and there is no evidence in his political theory – in contrast to his history of Florence – that the context in which he was writing was one of the great commercial centres of Europe. Yet there is a sense in which the spirit of his work is very much the spirit of the Italian commercial city, of Venice no less than of Florence, whose economic success was inextricably linked with military force. An ideology for such commercial powers, in which the city, governed by some kind of 'republican' collective of urban elites, was armed to dominate the *contado*, to suppress commercial rivals and expand the reach of its commercial supremacy, would have to be a blend of civic and military values, however much it was devoted to purely economic gain. As the commercial supremacy of the city-states waned, some critics blamed a decline in the warrior mentality of the urban elites.

The Dutch Republic

The Dutch Republic was probably the most commercialized society, not only in Europe but anywhere, before the advent of capitalism; and the Dutch constructed a huge commercial empire, much larger than the Venetian – extending from the Baltic to North America, and the East Indies to southern Africa – in which conquest for colonial settlement was a secondary, or auxiliary, concern. It is, for instance, indicative that the Dutch were leaders in the slave trade but far less dominant in the direct exploitation of slave plantations. Trade was the basic condition of Dutch life in unprecedented ways and to unparalleled degrees. In other non-capitalist societies, even those with well developed commercial economies, large sections of the population, often the majority, were peasants who supplied their own food needs and produced other necessary items at home, typically going to market only to supplement their basic survival strategies. In the maritime northern Netherlands, even farmers became dependent on trade for their basic food requirements,

especially grain, and sold other semi-luxury commodities – particularly dairy products and meat – in order to buy the basic necessities.
So the Dutch domestic economy was dependent to its very foundations on international trade, and this would generate a very strong
impulse to create a large commercial empire.[4]

As the ecological conditions of farming in the region made it
increasingly dependent on food grain from outside, the Dutch
developed their commercial apparatus to satisfy their own basic
needs. Crucially, they soon dominated the Baltic trade, which gave
them privileged access to cheap grain. In the process of providing for
their own needs, they became an essential link in the European
division of labour, and a major connection to the world outside
Europe. One result was massive urbanization, to service the needs of
the growing commercial economy, creating a proportion of urban to
rural population unmatched anywhere else in Europe. From the
sixteenth century, cities dominated Dutch society, and this dominance, in turn, shaped the rural economy.

Urbanization, fuelled by the Republic's role in international trade,
transformed the rural economy in at least two major ways. As the
urban population swelled to service the Republic's growing dominance in shipping, trade, and eventually finance, the growing urban
sector provided new markets for agricultural goods. At the same
time, it provided new sources of wealth to exploit new opportunities
for profit, and urban investors in agriculture became a major feature
of the rural scene. This was, in fact, a, if not the, critical factor in
transforming the Dutch rural economy, especially by means of
speculative urban investment in land reclamation.

The growth of cities, then, did not depend directly on agricultural
productivity. In a sense, the reverse was true. The cities grew because
of, and were sustained by, Dutch commercial development, the role
of the Dutch in the larger European system. This meant that cities

could expand well beyond the capacities of domestic agriculture to sustain them, as long as the external commercial opportunities were there. The wealth of those cities, which depended on commerce, was not limited by the constraints of domestic production. Urban development raised aggregate demand, which in turn encouraged the enhancement of agricultural productivity (assisted by urban capital), not so much to meet competitive conditions as to supply increasing demand, with a relatively small number of producers supplying an unusually large proportion of consumers.

This unprecedented degree of commercialization, and the penetration of trade relations into both urban and rural economies, may suggest a fairly well developed capitalism. Yet the Dutch Republic in many fundamental ways still operated on familiar non-capitalist principles, above all in its dependence on extra-economic powers of appropriation. In particular, its commercial dominance was not achieved in the manner of a capitalist enterprise, responding to cost-price pressures in a competitive market where advantage depends on increasing labour-productivity. Its supremacy, like that of earlier commercial empires, depended to a large extent on various kinds of extra-economic superiority, particularly in shipping and military technology. While it is true that Dutch merchants invested heavily in production, urban and rural, as long as ample market opportunities existed, and the Dutch pioneered many improvements in labour-productivity, not least in agriculture, it is not at all clear that they were driven by the kinds of competitive pressures associated with capitalism.

Agricultural productivity in the first instance seems to have been improved not under pressure of competition so much as in response to growing demand in an economy with a unique imbalance between urban consumers and rural producers, and continued in response to growing export markets, especially for luxury and semi-luxury goods.

More particularly, Dutch agricultural producers responded to the influence of low-cost economies, especially grain producers, not by competing with them but by using their own commercial dominance to gain advantage from foreign producers.

Dutch farmers originally shifted from grain to dairy production under the influence of cheap imported grain from the Baltic, because they were obtaining increasingly more grain for every pound of butter (as well as beef and cowhide) that they sold. Their privileged access to cheap grain – deriving from their extra-economic dominance in shipping and trade – was set against the prices of the 'relative luxuries' they themselves produced. Importing cheap grain lowered the costs of producing other, higher priced commodities at home. Dutch grain production, then, may have been replaced by lower cost 'competitors', but that 'competition' had the effect not of creating price/cost pressures or lowering profit margins in Dutch agriculture but, on the contrary, encouraging the production of higher priced and more profitable commodities. Low-cost production of grain elsewhere lowered the costs of inputs for Dutch producers, but not the price of their outputs, so their commercial dominance enabled them to enjoy the benefits of something like the opposite of the price/cost pressures that drive competitive production in a capitalist economy.

In other words, if the Dutch were subject to competition, it was less like capitalist price competition than extra-economic rivalry of a non-capitalist kind. Baltic grain, produced at costs determined by conditions in the region of origin, and especially in poorer locales, was bought and conveyed by Dutch merchants who enjoyed a clear dominance in the Baltic trade. That dominance had nothing to do with the costs of producing the traded commodity. The Dutch dominated the Baltic trade because they commanded the sea routes by means of superior shipping and naval power.

If Dutch prosperity in the 'Golden Age' of the Republic depended on a link between production and commerce, it was perhaps always a tenuous connection, and certainly a very mediated one, which may always have been vulnerable to rupture. To be sure, the Golden Age saw Dutch producers adapting themselves with considerable flexibility to changing conditions and transforming production to meet expanding commercial opportunities; and Dutch farmers continued to be remarkably flexible in their responses to economic change.[5] In their relative freedom to adapt production in this way they may indeed have been very different from peasant producers in other societies whose survival strategies have necessarily involved constraints on changes in production imposed by limited resources, or by customary practices, communal needs and regulations. But much of their success depended on the commercial role of the Republic and its merchants, whose connection with domestic production was, so to speak, always at one remove. When the European economy went into crisis in the late seventeenth century, and the market for luxury and semi-luxury goods contracted, Dutch commerce was increasingly detached from domestic production.

It has been argued that '[f]oreign trade rarely acts as the engine of growth of an economy', and that once the link between domestic production and international commerce was weakened, and the Dutch began to rely on their 'commercial sophistication' without a linkage to production at home, the economy was bound to cease growing and became 'less than the sum of its parts'.[6] But perhaps the reliance on commercial sophistication, as distinct from competitive production, was always essential to the Dutch economy. The commercial interests that dominated the economy were always, in a sense, semi-detached from domestic production and ready to shift their investments into other, often non-productive fields. Their vocation was, to put it simply, circulation, not production, and profit was generated by that means.

In this respect, the Dutch Republic was not unlike the commercial city-states of Italy. And here, too, as in other non-capitalist states – such as ancient empires and Italian city-states – public office was a major source of private wealth, a means of extracting surpluses from direct producers, urban and rural, to line the pockets of state officers. The proportion of such occupations in the population of Dutch cities was exceptionally high and exceedingly lucrative. When, after 1660, commercial opportunities began to dry up, the value of office as a source of wealth became even more evident and highly prized, and the governing elite of public office-holders in some places (notably Holland) had incomes higher than any other group. The largest total income was held by rentiers (a significant fact in itself), but 'no less than nine of the fifteen occupations with the highest average incomes were located in the public sector', including the top six occupations.[7]

Those who did not abandon commerce for office displayed a non-capitalist logic in other ways. The classic commercial interests of merchants whose profits derived from circulation rather than production asserted themselves more strongly than ever. They were likely to abandon domestic production for more lucrative means of trading in goods produced elsewhere, seeking to revive old monopolistic companies or even, as for instances in the case of one commercial enterprise, to gain a monopoly on navigational charts. In contrast to England, which responded to the declining European market by investing in cost-reducing innovations, the Dutch *dis*invested and reverted to, or intensified, non-capitalist forms of commerce or even 'extra-economic' appropriation, rentier wealth, and office-holding. The direction of Dutch economic development was determined not by the interests of competitive producers but by the needs of merchants and office-holders.

In its dependence on extra-economic power for economic gain, and in its extra-economic means of appropriation, the Dutch economy followed an essentially non-capitalist logic; and here, as elsewhere, military power was the bottom line. In the early years of the Dutch Republic, as it was coming into its golden age, military expenditures accounted for a greater proportion of the Republic's exceptionally high tax revenues than did any other activity, and the Dutch engaged in some notorious acts of aggression – the seizure of treasure-laden ships, for instance, or the massacre of rival merchants.[8] Although their superior shipping and navigation, as well as sophisticated financial instruments, often made it possible for the Dutch to dominate trade without coming into direct military confrontation with their rivals, military force was necessary to dominate trade routes, to enforce trade monopolies and to exclude rival states from various markets.

At first, the Dutch were primarily interested in access to trade routes and markets, throughout Europe and Asia, and in the ability of their merchants and trading companies like the Dutch East India Company to pursue their commercial interests aggressively. But as English and French rivals threatened their commercial supremacy, they became more interested in colonial settlement and embarked upon a programme of colonial conquest as ruthless as any other – though even here, the object was largely to facilitate trade. So, for instance, their settlements in southern Africa were founded for the purpose of provisioning commercial vessels. Military force was useful in other ways too – witness the role played by the Dutch in the English 'Glorious Revolution', which gave the English monarchy to the Dutch William of Orange and his wife, Mary. Whatever the English may have thought about their 'bloodless' revolution, the Dutch conceived it as an invasion, carried out with the support not only of the state but of the Amsterdam stock exchange, for purely commercial reasons, in an effort to counter the commercial rivalry of France by putting a reliable ally on the English throne.

The Dutch, then, perfected commercial imperialism, the principal object of which was not tribute, land, gold or even subject labour (though they certainly did not neglect these other advantages of empire) but supremacy in trade. While other commercial powers had engaged in imperial expansion to guarantee markets and trade routes, none had developed this formation to its ultimate limits, as did the Dutch. They also produced the perfect ideology of commercial imperialism – and this is worth a closer look, because it tells us a great deal about the logic of non-capitalist commercial imperialism. In later chapters, we shall have occasion to remark on the differences between the ideological requirements of capitalist imperialism and those of the most highly developed commercial empire.

The Ideology of Commercial Imperialism

The Dutch, in the person of Hugo Grotius (1583–1645), devised an ideology to match their 'extra-economic' means of establishing commercial supremacy.[9] Not surprisingly, this mode of imperial ideology above all took the form of a theory on the rights and wrongs of war. The case of Grotius is particularly important and revealing because he is commonly credited with founding international law, and his work is generally presented as a theory of *limitations* on war. Yet that work, in classics such as *Mare Liberum* and *De Jure Belli ac Pacis*, is striking for its ideological opportunism, transparently constructed to defend the very particular practices of the Dutch in their quest for commercial domination in the early seventeenth century.

Grotius himself had connections with the Dutch East India

Company; and while he was forced into exile from the Republic when the dominant faction with which he was associated was defeated by rivals, he never ceased to support the Dutch imperial project. To build his case, he not only produced a theory of war and peace but laid a foundation for transforming theories of politics and property in general.[10] If Grotius is indeed the founder of international law, we may have to admit that international law in its inception had as much to do with advocating as limiting war, and as much to do with profit as with justice.

Grotius was able to justify not only wars of self-defence, however broadly conceived, but even the most aggressive wars pursued for no other reason than commercial profit. In response to the traditional 'just war' requirement that a war can be just only if conducted by a proper authority, he sought to demonstrate that such authority could be vested not only in sovereign states but in private trading companies, which could legitimately engage in the most aggressive military acts to pursue their commercial advantage. In fact, the very principles commonly cited as central to his *restrictions* on war can have, and were intended to have, the opposite effect.

Grotius, like other theorists of the seventeenth century, is credited with something like a conception of the state of nature, according to which individuals possess natural rights prior to, and independent of, civil society. At the same time, states, which can have no powers that individuals do not already have in nature, must, he argued, like individuals be governed by the same moral principles. Although this is generally taken to place strict conditions on the rightful pursuit of war, this conception, with all its wide-ranging implications for political theory in general, was elaborated by Grotius (at a time when the Dutch were embarking on commercial expansion in the Indies) in order to defend aggressive military action, not just by states but by private traders – action such as the seizure of Portuguese ships –

on the grounds that individuals, like and even before states, have the right to punish those who wrong them. Grotius, as Richard Tuck puts it, 'made this remarkable claim, that there is no significant moral difference between individuals and states, and that both may use violence in the same way and for the same ends.'[11]

But violence in pursuit of commercial advantage, whether by states or private traders, does not, on the face of it, look like self-defence. So Grotius went further, effectively constructing a whole political theory on the principle that self-preservation is the first and most fundamental law of nature, and then defining self-preservation in the most capacious way. First, it means that individuals and states are permitted, perhaps even obliged, to acquire for themselves 'those things which are useful for life'. Although they may not, in the process, injure others who have not injured them, their own self-preservation comes first.

Grotius's notion of injury turns out to be very broadly permissive, while the moral principles to which individuals and states are both subject are minimal. The notion of some kind of international society bound together by certain common rules is regarded as one of Grotius's major contributions to international law and a peaceful world order. But his argument had far less to do with what individuals or states owe one another than with the right they have to punish each other in pursuit of self-interest, not only in defending themselves against attack, but 'proactively', as it were, in purely commercial rivalries. 'Grotius', concludes Tuck, 'endorsed for a state the most far-reaching set of rights to make war which were available in the contemporary repertoire.'[12]

This included not only a very wide-ranging international right of punishment but also, finally, a right to appropriate territory. To buttress that right, Grotius was obliged to develop a theory of property – and here, his ideological opportunism is particularly striking.

In the first instance, his main concern in constructing his theory of property was to argue for the freedom of the seas, to challenge the right of commercial rivals like the Portuguese to claim ownership of the seas and monopolize trade routes. We can only have a proprietary right, he maintained, to things we can individually consume or transform. The sea cannot be property, because, like air, it cannot be occupied or used in this way and is therefore a common possession. Furthermore, what cannot become private property, he argued (contrary to traditional conceptions of political jurisdiction), cannot, by the same token, be the public property of the state either, since both private and public ownership come about in the same way. No state jurisdiction is possible where the kind of control implied by property is impossible even in principle.

It is not difficult to see how military intervention might be justified on these grounds against those whose only wrong had been to assert a hitherto accepted right of state jurisdiction over neighbouring waters or the right to regulate certain fishing grounds and trade routes. Nor, of course, did this principle preclude the *de facto* monopolization of trade that the Dutch themselves were aiming for in certain places, where they simply coerced local populations into trade, establishing monopolies by forcing treaties on them, while aggressively repelling their European rivals.

At this point, Grotius was, in a sense, more concerned with what is *not* property than what is. For the purposes of defending Dutch commercial practices, and in particular, the actions of the East India Company, it was enough to insist on the freedom of the seas and the right to pursue commercial interests aggressively. But, as Tuck points out, the shift in Dutch commercial policy, in which trading companies became more interested in colonial settlement, inspired Grotius to mobilize his earlier theory of property to encompass this requirement too.

Having argued that something could become property only if it could be individually consumed or transformed, which might be true of land but not the sea, he now elaborated the other side of that argument: if usable things were left unused, there was no property in them, and hence people could appropriate land left unused by others. Grotius argued that no local authority could legitimately prevent free passage or the occupation of unused land, and any attempt to do so could legitimately be challenged by military means. Nevertheless, since land, unlike the sea, was in principle capable of transformation into property, it was also susceptible to political jurisdiction. Grotius never denied that indigenous authorities retained their general juris-diction over the land – something that Dutch trading companies effectively accepted by seeking the approval of these local authorities and even paying them for taking land out of their jurisdiction. But the basic principle remained: land left waste or barren – i.e. unculti-vated – was not property and could be occupied by those able and willing to cultivate it. Grotius's argument had clear affinities with the Roman law principle of *res nullius*, which decreed that any 'empty thing' such as unoccupied land was common property until it was put to use – in the case of land, especially agricultural use. This would become a common justification of European colonization.[13]

Grotius laid out a theory of politics, property and war that amply served the purposes of the world's most thoroughly commercial empire. But it would not suffice for a new kind of imperialism that was already emerging elsewhere. In the following chapters, we shall trace the development of a uniquely capitalist mode of imperialism, which demanded different practices and theories, such as even the most aggressive justifications of empire did not yet embrace.

4

A NEW KIND OF EMPIRE

All the major European empires made use of settler colonies to some extent, but white settler colonies were the essence of British imperialism in a way that was true of no other. The British, and particularly the English in the early days of the Empire, self-consciously regarded themselves as the first empire since Rome to succeed in enhancing imperial power by means of colonization. In the other European cases we have canvassed so far, empire was a matter of dominating trade, or a means of extracting precious resources, in large part by means of indigenous labour. While both these forms of imperialism, needless to say, required substantial degrees of colonial settlement, for the English colonization became an end in itself, and no other imperial power depended on white settler colonies to the same degree.

It was also England that first saw the emergence of a capitalist system, and it was England that first created a form of imperialism driven by the logic of capitalism. The combination of capitalist social property relations and the forceful expropriation of colonial territory may seem to contradict the proposition that capitalism is characterized by economic modes of appropriation, in contrast to the extra-economic forms that dominated non-capitalist societies. Colonization may seem a more ancient, less capitalist form of imperial power than is a commercial imperialism whose principle object is not the appropriation of territory but simply supremacy in trade. Yet it was English colonization, in contrast to Venetian or Dutch commercial imperialism, that was responding to the imperatives of capitalism.

Colonia

In 1516, Thomas More became, in his classic *Utopia*, the first major English writer to revive the ancient Roman concept of *colonia* to designate the settlement of foreign lands. The inhabitants of his Utopia would, he proposed, send out their surplus population to establish colonies in other territories. In Book II, More suggests that, ideally, occupying colonial land and making it fruitful would be to the advantage of both settlers and indigenous populations. But in some cases the colonists would, he argued, be justified in seizing territory by force, even if it required the coercive displacement of indigenous peoples. If local people were unwilling to join in the colonists' productive way of life, land not fruitfully used could rightfully be seized by those who would render it fruitful. In such cases, the colonists were entitled by natural law to appropriate land, without the permission (and here he goes further than Grotius would more than a century later) of any local authority:

> if there is any increase over the whole island, then they draw out
> a number of their citizens out of the several towns, and send them

over to the neighboring continent; where, if they find that the inhabitants have more soil than they can well cultivate, they fix a colony [*colonia*], taking the inhabitants into their society, if they are willing to live with them; and where they do that of their own accord, they quickly enter into their method of life, and conform to their rules, and this proves a happiness to both nations; for according to their constitution, such care is taken of the soil that it becomes fruitful enough for both, though it might be otherwise too narrow and barren for any one of them. But if the natives refuse to conform themselves to their laws, they drive them out of those bounds which they mark out for themselves, and use force if they resist. For they account it a very just cause of war, for a nation to hinder others from possessing a part of that soil of which they make no use, but which is suffered to lie idle and uncultivated; since every man has by the law of nature a right to such a waste portion of the earth as is necessary for his subsistence.

Later in the sixteenth century, England would embark upon a brutal colonial enterprise, justifying the forceful expropriation of local populations in much the same terms as More's utopian project. But the English would go even further, extending the principles outlined by More to encompass not just land unused or uncultivated altogether, but land not used fruitfully *enough*, and not in the right way, by the standards of English commercial agriculture.

This conception of colonization must be understood against the background of domestic developments in England. It was, after all, in England itself that the 'colonization' of land first took place in a form that would determine the direction of British imperial expansion. In the sixteenth century, there was a visible acceleration of a process that had been going on for some time, which would establish not only the principles of capitalist agriculture at home but also the logic of empire.

New land removed from the 'waste' and brought into cultivation, together with demesne land leased out by manorial lords, was increasingly subject to new forms of tenancy, different from the customary tenancies that had dominated relations between landlord and peasant and the relation of both to the land; and these new tenancies would increasingly submerge the older customary forms. Even customary leases often functioned according to the new principles, and old customary law which had placed restrictions on them was displaced by common law conceptions of exclusive private property. Leases no longer subject to the restrictions of rents fixed by custom were made responsive to the market. Landlords could vary rents according to market conditions, and they could make 'improvement' of land a condition of leases, which was likely to make them accessible only to already successful farmers who could undertake improvement, to enhance productivity and profit. This did not necessarily mean that rents would be very high – although the trend would be upward as land was improved. A balance could be struck between giving a tenant sufficient security to encourage improvement, and exacting a good rent (and often what amounted to the purchase of the lease in the form of an entry fine) from prosperous tenants. These tenants would, in turn, often employ wage labour – establishing the famous 'triad' of capitalist agriculture, the network of landlord, capitalist tenant and wage labourer – and the number of available labourers would grow, as small producers went to the wall and land was increasingly concentrated in the hands of 'improving' landlords and their commercially successful tenants.

As landlords lost their extra-economic powers to an increasingly centralized state, a process accelerated by the Tudor monarchy, their wealth increasingly depended on the productivity and commercial success of their tenants. This, in turn, increased the pressure to concentrate land in the hands of landlords and more successful farmers, who would have the capital and the flexibility to make the most profitable use of the land. With that pressure, the enclosure of common land or open fields by communal agreement, or by exchanges among smallholders, gave way to a more coercive process of extinguishing customary rights, driving small producers off the land and excluding the community from regulation of production. Even without coercive eviction, customary tenures were increasingly replaced by economic leases and competitive rents. The increasing polarization between successful capitalist farmers and customary tenants operating on older principles hastened – by purely economic means – the displacement of smaller producers with inflexible rents and neither the means nor the incentive to produce competitively.

Although these processes were long in the making, the sixteenth century, as R.H. Tawney pointed out long ago, marks the culmination of a transition from 'the mediaeval conception of land as the basis of political functions and obligations to the modern view of it as an income-yielding investment.'[1] While feudal lords had depended on their command of men, both for labour and for military service, the new type of landlord was increasingly dependent on the commercial profits generated by his land. His land agents and surveyors became ever more preoccupied with measuring the purely economic value of land – the market rents it could command, as against customary rents or the obligatory labour services that had once constituted the principal value of land to its lordly owners.

The new relations between landlords and tenants inevitably affected their relation to the land and the meaning of property itself. As the productivity and profitability of agriculture became essential concerns of both landlords and their tenants, claims to land increasingly came to depend on its 'improvement', its productive and profitable use – first, in the sense that success in commercial agriculture gave farmers privileged access to more and better land;

then, in the sense that even legal property rights were subject to the same requirements. Improvement, for instance, could be the decisive consideration in legal disputes over enclosure. Such conceptions of property rights were rooted in new principles of value, and these would eventually develop from the rudimentary calculations of the land surveyor, measuring the 'unearned' increment enjoyed by customary tenants who paid less than a market rent, to elaborate economic theories in which value was created in production and not just derived from unequal commercial exchange.

This, then, was the logic of agrarian capitalism, which was gradually enveloping the English countryside; and with it came new principles of imperial expansion. The history of early agrarian capitalism – the process of domestic 'colonization', the removal of land from the 'waste', its 'improvement', enclosure and new conceptions of property rights – was reproduced in the theory and practice of empire.

The Colonization of Ireland

It is a striking fact that, despite its navigational skills, England was a slow starter in the European race for commercial supremacy. When it did seriously embark on overseas expansion, it certainly did so not least to ensure commercial access for its merchants and trading companies; but by that time its internal economic development had given rise to other principles of empire. The 'laboratories' of this new Empire were not overseas but closer to home, in the border regions of the British Isles and, above all, in Ireland.[2]

'The most potent lesson demonstrated by the Irish experience,' writes one historian of the British Empire in Ireland, 'is that the establishment of colonies of settlement, on the model of those of the

Romans, was feasible in the modern world, and the most distinctive feature of the future British Empire within the spectrum of European overseas empires is the prominent place enjoyed by colonies of white settlement within it.'³ He could have added that the most potent lesson demonstrated by the English agrarian experience at home was that colonial settlement was possible in the modern world on a new footing.

In the late sixteenth century, in the face of disorder and rebellion in Ireland, the Tudor state embarked on a brutal new project of colonization. What was new about this project was not that it mobilized a public/private partnership by encouraging private colonists to settle there. Ireland had long been settled by English lords, and the state, such as it was in the middle ages, had relied to a great extent on more or less feudal military lords to subdue 'the wild Irish'. But by the sixteenth century, this feudal mode of imperial rule had failed as a means of colonial dominance; and attempts to impose order by incorporating Ireland into the English state were clearly not working, not least because old English lordly families claimed control over their territories and enforced it with their own military power. War and theft among the English lords was itself a constant threat to order. To establish control over both Irish and old (Catholic) English, the Tudor monarchy, as it consolidated the English state at home, launched a much more aggressive policy of colonization, which would be 'the chief legacy of late Elizabethan Ireland to English colonization in the New World.'⁴

The object was certainly conquest, but military conquest would not be enough. Nor would the English rely upon simply imposing their government and law upon the recalcitrant Irish. The policy was not just to impose English rule but to transform Irish society itself by means of 'plantation', the settlement of English and Scottish colonists who would undertake to make the land fruitful. The stated intention was to reproduce the social property relations of south-east England, introducing the form of landlord–tenant relation that had been establishing itself in the English countryside, with the object of reproducing English commercial agriculture. The effect would be not only to 'civilize' the Irish but also, or so it seems was the intention, to absorb Ireland into the English economy, making it into a dependency in a way that attempts at political and legal integration had so far failed to do.

On the eve of this new colonial programme, areas of Ireland already dominated by the English had to some extent introduced English agriculture. But the policy now was a wholesale transformation of agrarian relations, even, or especially, in areas still dominated by indigenous social relations and practices. The English would seek to eradicate the Irish system of property in favour of English-style commercial tenancies, and replace what has been called a 'consumption-oriented redistributive economy' with a commercial one, driven by market imperatives.[5] Irish overlords, as well as English lords, who used their extra-economic power to exact tribute from those under their authority, would be replaced by landlords whose wealth was derived from rents generated by tenants engaged in productive commercial agriculture. These effects would be achieved above all by large-scale expropriation and displacement of the Irish, and land grants to Englishmen and Scots, although some Irish lords would retain their land by becoming 'improving' landlords themselves and even taking English and Scottish tenants.

The first major plantation of this kind was in Munster beginning in the 1580s, which involved a very large number of settlers and a huge transfer of land from the Irish to English and Scottish colonists. When the Tudor state faced the greatest challenge to its authority in the province of Ulster, it set in train, in the early seventeenth century, an even more comprehensive effort to transform Ireland by means of plantation and land grants to Englishmen and Scots, as well as loyal Irishmen. The results were enormously profitable for these 'improving' landlords.

The Ulster Plantation produced one of the most revealing documents of England's early colonial ventures. Sir John Davies, a lawyer, statesman and writer who was one of the principal architects of English imperialism in Ireland, had a particularly vicious view of the Irish and was very keen to subdue them by conquest and outright expulsion or transplantation. He justified the Ulster Plantation by invoking, for instance, the transplantation of Moors in Spain, or troublesome clans from the Scottish Borders. But he also offered a more telling justification.

In a letter to the Earl of Salisbury in 1610, having argued that the king has supreme rights over the land not only by English common law but by Irish customary law (which was, in any case, no law at all but just 'lewd' and 'unreasonable' custom), Davies went on to insist that the king was not only entitled by law but bound in conscience to seize Irish land:

> ... His Majesty is bound in conscience to use all lawful and just courses to reduce his people from barbarism to civility; the neglect whereof heretofore hath been laid as an imputation upon the Crown of England. Now civility cannot possibly be planted among them by this mixed plantation of some of the natives and settling of their possessions in a course of Common Law; for if themselves were suffered to possess the whole country, as their septs have done for many hundred of years past, they would never, to the end of the world, build houses, make townships or villages, or manure or improve the land as it ought to be; therefore it stands neither with Christian policy nor conscience to suffer so good and fruitful a country to lie waste like a wilderness,

when his Majesty may lawfully dispose it to such persons as will make a civil plantation thereupon.

Again, his majesty may take this course in conscience because it tendeth to the good of the inhabitants many ways; for half their land doth now lie waste, by reason whereof that which is habited is not improved to half the value; but when the undertakers [the settlers] are planted among them . . ., and that land shall be fully stocked and manured, 500 acres will be of better value than 5000 are now.

This passage is reminiscent of Thomas More, but it already goes a significant step beyond even More's fairly uncompromising justification of colonial expropriation without the agreement of local authorities, let alone the old Roman principle of *res nullius* and the right to claim unoccupied land. The criterion for Davies is not simply the lack of occupation, or even the lack of cultivation. The decisive issue is *value*, understood in a specifically English sense. Irish lands can be expropriated, not because they are unoccupied (which they are not), nor even because they are uncultivated (which they are not), but because they are not fruitful and profitable by the standards of English commercial agriculture. Their value is less than one tenth of what it would be by means of English-style improvement.

It is impossible to overestimate the significance of this conceptual move. It testifies to the new principles of property already introduced into the English countryside and now invoked as a justification of empire. No longer is empire simply a means of subjecting populations for the purposes of tax and tribute or the extraction of precious resources. Nor is it simply a means of ensuring commercial supremacy by controlling the networks of trade. We can observe here the transition from commercial conceptions of profit – the profits of unequal exchange, 'buying cheap' and 'selling dear' – to capitalist profit, the profit derived from competitive production, from the increased productivity enabled by 'improvement'. And with these new conceptions of property and profit come new forms of, and new reasons for, colonization. If, as Tawney said, sixteenth-century England marked a clear transition from medieval conceptions of land as a source of labour services and military force to land as a profit-making investment, much the same can be said about the mode of empire pioneered by the English in Ireland.

The Value of Empire

The same principles would be at work in Oliver Cromwell's even more brutal conquest several decades later. By that time, England had a much more effective fighting force, a standing army that may have been the best in Europe. In response to Irish rebellion, Cromwell mobilized these forces with a vengeance. The object, again, was to dispossess Irish landholders and replace them with colonial settlers, this time with an even more wholesale expulsion of Catholic proprietors. Some Catholics would be permitted to keep small pieces of land west of the Shannon, but their access to the sea and foreign contact was to be blocked by a colony of soldier-settlers.

This massive exercise in colonization was designed to transform the whole of Irish society more completely than ever before, and this required elaborate planning. The most important condition was a land survey, the Down Survey, conducted by Cromwell's Surveyor General, William Petty, which gave Ireland 'the doubtful distinction of being the most accurately surveyed and mapped country in Europe'.[6] Petty, who would later be regarded by many as the founder of classical political economy, set out not only to map the land but to value it, for the purpose of distributing it equitably among

Cromwell's soldiers and others who had contributed to the colonial enterprise, as well as for fiscal purposes. He introduced his own original criteria of valuation, which created a theoretical foundation for capitalist conceptions of value that were already appearing in practice. Beginning as a method of valuing land, it would also underpin England's trade policy; and with the theory of value came the new capitalist 'science' of political economy.

In his effort to assess the relative profitability of land, to determine not only distribution but the appropriate rents and taxes attached to any piece of land, Petty maintained that value could not simply be determined by more or less accidental commercial exchanges, the 'bargains which a few men make one with another, through ignorance, haste, false suggestion, or else passion or drink.'[7] In the first instance, it would be necessary to measure the 'intrinsick value' of land, the full measure of the commodities it could produce – for example, the weight of hay one piece of land could produce as against another. But a further step was needed to enable commercial transactions, which required some constant means of measuring the 'extrinsick value' of commodities in monetary terms. Here, Petty introduced a major innovation that would deeply affect the development of political economy. The common standard of measurement between two completely different commodities – a bushel of hay, for instance, against the silver needed to pay for it – was the labour required to produce them. This determined the 'natural' price and also allowed an estimate of the appropriate rent.

Petty would not stop at measuring the value of land. He also, in *The Political Anatomy of Ireland* in 1691, computed the comparative value of human beings in improved as against unimproved societies. Starting from a value comparable to the price of African slaves – at £25 for an adult male – Petty estimated that the improvement of Ireland, under the auspices of an imperial power whose objective was to transform the Irish into a completely different people, could raise the value of an Irishman to that of an Englishman, worth £70.

Petty's 'labour theory of value' bespeaks an economy in which profit is generated not simply by commercial exchange, the 'bargains which a few men make', but by competitive production. Petty, like others among his contemporaries, was interested in economic policies primarily aimed 'at securing the most efficient deployment of human and material resources. . . . They realised that it was no longer possible to maintain a system based on a monopoly of expensive cloth exports to various parts of Europe. Their economic policies emphasised competitive cheapness, economic diversification and the expansion of trade outside Europe.'[8] 'To provide for the poore, advance trade and make all manufactures flourish,' Petty wrote,

> England should bee endeavoured to bee made the shop of Europe, and it with other countries the markets. To doe this all trades and workmen should bee encouraged and all manner of compendious ways invented wherby they may come to undersel the manufactures and commodities of all other countrys. This would bee better then to strengthen their monopolizing corporations in ignorance and idleness.[9]

This emphasis on competitive cheapness, as distinct from non-capitalist methods of ensuring commercial dominance by extra-economic means, and the premium it placed on cost-effective production, affected not only economic development at home but the logic of imperial expansion. The expectation was not only that colonists would adopt new methods of production but also that colonial products and raw materials could be exploited to provide the means of improving competitive production at home.

Before the industrialization of Britain could absorb a large domestic labour force, the growing mass dispossessed by agrarian capitalism provided a surplus population for colonial expansion, in a way, for instance, that the peasant society of France never did. In this way, too, the domestic development of capitalist agriculture fueled colonization and helps to explain why, of all the major European powers, England had the most success in recruiting colonial settlers. Economic development at home would eventually provide more employment for Britain's dispossessed, and the labour supply in the colonies would be notoriously supplemented by slavery on a massive scale.

The colonies, then, could help to maintain social order at home, while enhancing England's commercial supremacy by increasing its competitive advantage. The principal object, of course, was to increase the wealth of the English by creating exploitable dependencies, not to spawn potential competitors in the colonies. In Ireland, for instance, the English state took measures to block commercial development as soon as it showed signs of offering serious competition to the imperial power. This was just the first of many instances in which the irreducible contradictions of capitalism – such as the contradiction between its drive to expand the market imperatives of competition and its need to resist competition, or between its need for increasing demand and its tendency to restrict demand by impoverishing dispossessed and exploited populations – made themselves felt in colonial policy. In this way and others, the development of Ireland has, needless to say, been shaped ever since by its early colonial history of conquest, expropriation, and the polarization between the mass of dispossessed and an imperial elite with its indigenous allies.

Petty's distinction between, on the one hand, the practice of gaining economic ascendancy by means of commercial monopolies, and, on the other, innovative and competitive production to 'undersel' all others, nicely sums up the differences between non-capitalist patterns of commercial imperialism and the new conception of empire. The English, as we shall see, would never again be able, in any other settler colony, to reproduce England's distinctive property relations, however much they would have liked to universalize their forms of tenancy or the 'triad' of landlord, tenant and wage labourer. But the new imperialism would continue to provide opportunities for profitable production in the colonies and inputs for domestic production, as well as a safety valve for the surplus labour(ers) created by increasing labour productivity.

It is instructive here to contrast, in the persons of Petty and Grotius, the case of England's new imperial venture with the most highly developed commercial empire emanating from the Dutch Republic. While the Dutch certainly pioneered many advances in production, it remains a telling fact that their most notable theoretical contribution to imperialism, the body of thought most expressive of the Republic's commercial empire, was a philosophy of war and peace and a theory of relations among states, not the political economy of competitive production.

Yet the new kind of empire, however much it presented itself as the peaceful pursuit of production and trade, was at least as violent as any other. England did not, of course, abandon the extra-economic rivalries that determined commercial supremacy among the European powers. On the contrary, Britain would increasingly depend on a massive naval force to impose its domination over international networks of trade. The new logic of capitalist appropriation by means of competitive production did lay a foundation for economic competition as an alternative to extra-economic rivalry, and economic imperatives as an alternative to direct colonial rule; but it would be a very long time before economic imperatives were widespread and powerful enough to reduce the need for direct colonial coercion and command of trade by military means. At the same time, the new mode of appropriation created wholly new needs for military violence, not least in pursuit of colonial settlements – and capitalism has continued ever since to spawn new forms of war and generate new reasons for it.

5

THE OVERSEAS EXPANSION OF ECONOMIC IMPERATIVES

Capitalism is uniquely driven by economic imperatives: on the one hand, the propertylessness of producers, which compels them to sell their labour power for a wage, and, on the other, the subjection of appropriators to the compulsions of the market, which oblige them to compete and accumulate. But these economic imperatives require extra-economic force to implant and sustain them. The transplantation of economic imperatives from England to its imperial territories first took place by means of forcible colonial expropriation and settlement. The effect of capitalist imperatives emanating from the imperial homeland is, above all, what distinguished British imperialism from other colonial projects; and, whatever debates there may be among historians about the contribution of empire to the development of British capitalism, it seems indisputable that the development of capitalism at home in Britain determined the shape of British imperialism.

The testing ground for the new form of empire, as we have seen, was Ireland; and the Irish experience informed the effort to extend the reach of England's economy beyond the British Isles, across the seas. The pattern of colonization in America was meant to be something like the settlement of Ireland, but different circumstances meant that it would soon depart from the Irish pattern. Not the least significant difference was that the expropriation of indigenous peoples was even more complete. Here it meant not only the appropriation of their land but, eventually, their removal altogether. With few exceptions, there were to be no indigenous landlords, tenants or even labourers; and transplantation became genocide. At the same time, the unique conditions in this vast expanse of land meant that imposing English social property relations, and economic imperatives emanating from the imperial homeland, was not a simple matter even among colonists. This experiment, profitable as it was for a time, would end in war with the colonies, which the imperial power famously lost.

Britain would encounter different, almost antithetical, problems in its so-called 'second' Empire and especially in India. Here, in this densely populated territory, with a highly developed economy and elaborate political arrangements, there was not even the remotest possibility of domination primarily by means of white settler colonies, despite the extent of colonial settlement; and, in any case, the commercial and productive development of India attracted Britain's imperial ambitions for rather different reasons than had Ireland or America in the early days of colonization. The irony is that, in these conditions, Britain seemed, on the face of it, to revert to earlier, non-capitalist forms of empire: the commercial imperialism of the East India Company, and then a territorial empire presided over by the British state. There was a constant tension between the imperatives of capitalism and the demands of territorial imperialism, which would continue to shape the British Empire till the end.

Empire as Property

It is not uncommon to contrast the Spanish mode of colonization with both the English and French, as if the latter two represented simply variants of a single form of empire. We are told, for instance, that the English and French were interested in commerce and agriculture, and set out to cultivate the land in America, while the Spanish 'had gone to occupy and to benefit, as all good noblemen did, from the labour of others.'[1] This is the primary reason for the absence of the *res nullius* principle in Spanish justifications of empire, in contrast to both English and French. While their imperial rivals were interested in claims to land, the Spanish were at least as concerned with command over people and labour. This meant, as we have seen, that they freely admitted to an empire of conquest, legitimated by the doctrine of 'just war', while the English and French found their legitimation in justifying occupation of unused and unfruitful land.

But the difference between French and English patterns of settlement in North America, and especially the effects they had on local populations, is, in its way, as significant as the difference between either one and Spanish colonization. The divergence is visible not only in their different relations to the indigenous population but even in their varying conceptions of *res nullius*; and it points to some essential distinctions between commerce and capitalism.

The settlement of the Americas by the main imperial rivals, Spain, France and England, has been summed up as follows: 'Unlike the French and the English, who first settled among the Indian population before they attempted either to integrate them as the French had done or exterminate them like the English, the Spaniards were committed, even by the terms of the capitulations made to Columbus in 1492, to extensive occupation.'[2]

These differences were no doubt in part determined by what the imperial powers found in their various colonies and particularly the great variations among the indigenous populations, in the levels of resistance they presented and also in the possibilities of profitable exploitation. Spain, unlike England and France, not only found the riches of gold and silver mines but encountered densely populated and sedentary civilizations with highly organized states, as well as material and technological achievements in many ways more advanced than its own. To be sure, the devastating effects of disease brought by the Europeans drastically weakened the resistance of all the indigenous peoples, in the south as in the north; and in that sense, the opposition faced by conquerors was everywhere diluted. But relations between conquerors and conquered were affected by irreducible differences in the purposes of colonization – between the French and the English, no less than between both and the Spanish – which cannot be accounted for simply by the variations in conditions on the ground.

The Spanish, as we have seen, were primarily concerned with the extraction of gold and silver, so they had an interest in exploiting the labour and technical capabilities of indigenous peoples in their South American colonies, in mines as well as on plantations. That certainly accounts in large part for a policy which, however brutal, was not intended to wipe out the local population. The primary interest of France in America was the fur trade; and in this, the indigenous peoples were necessary partners. At the same time, this kind of commercial expansion did not, like colonization of land for agricultural production, require or encourage a massive wave of colonial settlers – and, in any case, France, with its peasant majority at home, had not produced a surplus population like the English dispossessed by agrarian capitalism. When, in the seventeenth century, the French state embarked on a systematic effort to settle New France, if only to counter the English threat to French domination of the fur trade, it did so by creating quasi-feudal *seigneuries*. This was also the time when France, under the guidance of Colbert and Richelieu, was engaged in its domestic project of creating a unified centralized state, with a standardized language and culture. Their programme of colonization was meant to extend this process into the colonies, with the intention of supplementing the inadequate colonial settlements with Frenchified Indians, even intermarried with the colonists. This project of unification, cultural assimilation and religious conversion ultimately failed; but, while French relations with the Indians have their own destructive history, they never descended into the genocidal brutality of the English colonization.

The English encountered native populations more similar to those in the French colonies than in the Spanish, and certainly nothing like the empires of Latin America. But, while they too engaged in the fur trade, their imperial purposes were generally quite different from the French. If English colonial settlers in America had ever intended to live side-by-side with indigenous people, they soon relinquished that intention and set out systematically to displace the local population. The nature of this colonial settlement made that outcome inevitable. Had the English colonists, like the French, been primarily interested in older forms of trade and trading posts, they might have preserved relatively peaceful, or at least less genocidal, relations with the Indians, and there might have been a greater intermingling of the populations. But, as it became increasingly clear that the object of colonization was, above all, the appropriation and permanent settlement of land, a long and bloody confrontation between settlers and indigenous peoples was a foregone conclusion.

To explain this fairly dramatic difference between English and French colonial settlement, it is not enough simply to invoke, for instance, English Puritanism and its conviction that it was doing divine work in replacing the 'savagery' of heathens with the 'godliness' of English settlers, even if it meant exterminating 'savages'. Nor is it enough to point out that the English needed land for its surplus population in a way that France did not. This was certainly a significant factor, but it also testifies to differences between French and English social property relations at home, which played out their logic in other ways too.

We can arrive at some understanding of the divergences by considering how the English and the French conceived the *res nullius* principle, the notion that unoccupied or unused land could rightfully be appropriated by those who would render it fruitful. Here is how, even in the eighteenth century, the principle was delineated in 1758 by Emeric de Vattel, in his *Le Droit de gens ou principe de la loi naturelle*, 'which became the textbook account of the nature of natural rights of property in the second half of the eighteenth century':[3]

The cultivation of the soil not only deserves attention of a government because of its great utility, but in addition is an obligation imposed upon man by nature. Every nation is therefore bound by natural law to cultivate the land which has fallen to its share. . . . Those peoples such as the Ancient Germans and certain modern Tartars who, though dwelling in fertile countries, disdain the cultivation of the soil and prefer to live by plunder, fail in their duty to themselves, injuring their neighbours, and deserve to be exterminated like wild beasts of prey. . . . Thus while the conquest of the civilized empires of Peru and Mexico was a notorious usurpation, the establishment of various colonies upon the continent of North America might, if it be done within just limits, be entirely lawful. The people of these vast tracts of land rather roamed over them than inhabited them.[4]

This was written long after France had supplemented its pursuit of the fur trade with a major project of settlement; and, on the face of it, this statement is as permissive in its legitimation of colonial expropriation as any imperialist could wish. It would certainly have allowed extensive colonization of the Americas, if not in the 'civilized empires of Peru and Mexico' (conquered, of course, by the brutal Spanish, unlike their civilized French and English rivals), then certainly wherever indigenous populations supported themselves primarily by means of hunting–gathering rather than by agricultural production. Although Vattel took issue with Grotius for his excessive bellicosity and the lengths he was willing to go to in justifying punitive wars, he certainly agreed with Grotius about the legitimacy of colonization;[5] and it is not clear that his argument required even the token permission demanded by Grotius.

Yet Vattel did not in essence move beyond the most ancient understanding of the principle that unused land was open to appropriation for the purpose of making it fruitful. The 'just limits' he invoked, however permissive, drew the line of lawful colonization between land inhabited and settled by indigenous people, which could not be legitimately expropriated, and land over which they simply 'roamed', which was fair game to colonial settlers. The Indians had no right to the whole of the huge North American continent, and certainly no right to what they did not cultivate. But that they had *some* rights seems not to have been in dispute. In this respect, this eighteenth-century Frenchman did not go as far as the English had already done in the seventeenth century, when they redefined the 'just limits' of colonization beyond anything that had ever been claimed by England's rivals.

The English, as we have seen, were already in the early seventeenth century operating, both at home and in Ireland, with a principle of rightful appropriation, indeed expropriation, that embraced not only occupied but even cultivated land. Later in the century that principle would receive a more systematic and theoretical elaboration at the hands of John Locke. Like Petty before him, Locke constructed his theory on a conception of value, and like Petty, he attributes the value of a thing to the labour embodied in it. But, while Petty had developed a labour theory of value simply in order to measure the value of land for distribution and taxation – which, although certainly intended as an instrument of empire, did not itself supply a justification of colonization – Locke devised a labour theory of *property*, which could justify not only eviction or enclosure at home but also colonial expropriation.

In effect, Locke provided a theoretical structure for the principle already enunciated by Sir John Davies in Ireland: that the essential criterion in the justification of colonial expropriation was *value*, and that value was to be judged against the standard of English 'improvement'. For Locke, America was the model state of nature, in which all land was available for appropriation, because, although it was certainly inhabited and even sometimes cultivated, there was no proper commerce, hence no 'improvement', no productive and profitable use of the land, and therefore no real property. As Davies had done in Ireland, Locke contrasted the 'value' of unimproved land in America to the vastly greater value of land in England. That huge difference was determined not by any variation in the 'intrinsic' value of land in the two cases – its fertility and natural quality – but rather by the exchange-value created in production, which depended not only on improvements in production but on the existence of a commercial system that impelled such improvements and generated profit. The creation of value established a right of property where no individual property had existed before. This theory of property justified at one and the same time the practices of colonialists in the Americas and of capitalist landlords at home, interests combined perfectly in the person of Locke's mentor, the first Earl of Shaftesbury.

Commentators have pointed out that Locke introduced an important innovation into the *res nullius* principle by justifying colonial appropriation of unused land without the consent of any local sovereign, and that he provided settlers with an argument that justified their actions on the basis of natural law, without any reference to civil authority.[6] In that respect, he went even further than Grotius, with his equivocal recognition of local authority – although, here, Locke did have a precursor in Thomas More, as we have seen. But there is something even more distinctive in Locke's argument, which owes less to pan-European legal and philosophical traditions than to the specific experience of England, and to its domestic property relations even before its colonial ventures.

Like Grotius, Locke associates property with use and transformation. But his argument is not simply that things can become property when, and only when, they are used and transformed. The point is rather that the right of property derives from the creation of value. His famous labour theory of property in Chapter Five of his *Second Treatise of Government*, according to which we acquire property in something when we 'mix' our labour with it, is full of complexities (including the question of *whose* labour, since the master is entitled to property derived from his servant's labour), which there is no space to explore here. But one thing that is emphatically clear is that the creation of value is the basis of property. Labour establishes a right of property because it is labour that '*puts the difference of value on every thing*' (#40). And the value in question is not 'intrinsic' but *exchange* value.

This implies not only that mere occupancy is not enough to establish property rights, or even that hunting–gathering cannot establish the right of property while agriculture can, but also that insufficiently productive and profitable agriculture, by the standards of English agrarian capitalism, effectively constitutes waste. Land in America is open to colonization, Locke argues, because an acre of land in 'unimproved' America, which may be as naturally fertile as an acre in England, and have the same 'intrinsick' (*sic*) value, is not worth 1/1000 of the English acre, if we calculate 'all the Profit an *Indian* received from it were it valued and sold here' (#43). This may not mean that a more productive use will always trump the less productive (though, in practice, that would be the effect of competitive production); and, once taken out of common possession, individual property cannot simply be seized for more profitable use. But it does mean that when, as in the case of Amerindians (at least in Locke's understanding), there is no proper commerce and hence no improvement, there is no property; and any land left in this state is available for appropriation. This would apply not only to land roamed by hunter–gatherers but to cultivated land worked by Indians, like many of those encountered by the English colonists.

Locke thus goes beyond even Grotius in asserting the primacy of private property over political jurisdiction in the colonies. In fact, political jurisdiction at either end of the colonial relationship is conspicuously absent. Locke does invoke a theory of 'just war' for the purpose of justifying slavery, as others before him had done, arguing that captives taken in a war legitimately waged can rightfully be enslaved; yet his theory of colonization is not a theory of war or international law but a theory of private property, which applies both at home and abroad. His discussion of conquest and war elsewhere in the *Second Treatise* does suggest (as More's *Utopia* had done) that unimproved land can be the object of just war. But it is no small matter that this major and most innovative English contribution to the justification of empire is a theory of property rights. Locke's theory of colonial appropriation rests on something other than the question of political jurisdiction or the right of one political power to dominate another. At the same time, if he is more interested in property than in relations among states, he goes far beyond earlier theories that justified colonization as legitimate appropriation, whether based on *res nullius* or papal donation. Instead, he grounds colonial expansion in a new, and essentially capitalist, conception of property. In his theory of property, we can observe imperialism becoming a directly *economic* relationship, even if that relationship required brutal force to implant and sustain it. That kind of relationship could be justified not by the right to rule, nor even simply the right to appropriate, but by the right, indeed the obligation, to produce exchange-value.

For Grotius, writing on behalf of the Dutch commercial empire – in which the principal issue was commercial rivalry among trading nations vying for supremacy in international commerce – it really was a question of 'international relations', above all the issue of war and peace among states. Although the Dutch certainly introduced innovations in their own domestic production, the kind of commercial supremacy they enjoyed depended in large part on 'extra-economic' advantages, superior shipping and sophisticated commercial practices, the command of sea routes, *de facto* if not always *de jure* trading monopolies, and far-flung trading posts. All of these advantages were, in one way or another, bound up with questions of war, peace, military might and diplomacy. Even when the Dutch supplemented their earlier policies of imposing trade on local powers, in the Indies and elsewhere, with outright colonial settlement, so that Grotius was obliged to extend his argument to encompass colonial appropriation, he never gave up his original conceptual framework, just as the Dutch never gave up their primary concern with trade and commercial supremacy.

Early modern England, no less than other commercial powers,

engaged in the same international rivalries; and, needless to say, the expansion of the British Empire would continue to require massive military force and particularly a powerful navy. But there was already something new in both the theory and practice of empire, and we find its best early expression in Locke. Here, we see the beginnings of a conception of empire rooted in capitalist principles, in pursuit of profit derived not simply from exchange but from the creation of value in competitive production. This is a conception of empire that is not simply about establishing imperial rule or even commercial supremacy but about extending the logic and the imperatives of the domestic economy and drawing others into its orbit. Although capitalist imperialism would never dispense with more traditional means of justifying imperial expansion, it had now added wholly new weapons to the ideological arsenal, just as it had pioneered new social property relations, which had their effects both in the domestic economy and in the strategies of imperial expansion.

Economic justifications of empire would never, of course, be enough. From the beginning, for instance, the English resorted to portraying the Irish or the Amerindians as, for one reason or another, inferior beings. But even when defences of imperialism had recourse to such extra-economic ideologies, they were deeply affected by capitalism's reliance on economic imperatives. Because capitalist class exploitation takes the form of a market relation, it cannot easily be justified by invoking hierarchies of civic or legal status, such as the relation between feudal lords and serfs. Instead, the relation between capital and labour is typically presented as a contractual relation between legally free and equal individuals. This reliance on purely economic modes of exploitation, and the suppression of extra-economic identities and hierarchies, has, in fact, made capitalism compatible with ideologies of civic freedom and equality in a way that non-capitalist class systems never were. These ideologies can even be mobilized to justify the capitalist system, as the epitome of freedom and equality. Yet, at least for a time, when ideologies of civic freedom and equality confronted the realities of imperialism and slavery, the effect was to place a new premium on racism, as a substitute for all the other extra-economic identities that capitalism had displaced.

The unavailability of old ascriptive categories and hierarchies, such as the differences of legal status which defined feudal relations, meant that imperialism and slavery had to be justified by other means. In non-capitalist societies, there had existed a wide spectrum of dependent conditions – not only, or even primarily, slavery, but also debt bondage, serfdom, peonage and so on – all of which were defined by various forms of legal or political dependency and status hierarchies. Capitalism increasingly displaced that spectrum of dependent labour. Yet, for a time, as juridical dependence disappeared in relations among Englishmen, as well as among colonists, but before the advent of a mass proletariat to provide a concentrated and intensively exploitable 'free' labour force, there was an increasing demand for dependent labour from outside the imperial community, in sectors requiring intensive exploitation – as in the large-scale colonial production of highly marketable commodities like tobacco and sugar or cotton. All that remained in the spectrum of dependent labour was chattel slavery; and, if now discarded ideologies of legal status hierarchy could no longer be invoked, some other justification had to be found. The result was that a new ideological role was assigned to pseudo-biological conceptions of race, which excluded certain human beings, not simply by law but by nature, from the normal universe of freedom and equality.

The British in America

English colonists had for some time before Locke been operating in America according to the principles he later elaborated – not least in the sense that they pushed Indians even out of cultivated land. But how the land was held and used varied greatly among colonies and regions, depending not only on the nature of the settlers and the land grants they received but also on the quality of the land and the crops it could sustain.

The logic of Britain's domestic capitalism would not play itself out in the same ways and degrees everywhere in North America, and we shall concentrate here on the cases in which that logic is most clearly visible, the colonies of the future United States. British North America, the empire in Canada, was in some ways an anomaly. On the one hand, it was never particularly profitable for the imperial power, once it became a settler colony rather than simply a massive trading post; on the other, though a white settler colony like others in the British Empire, it lasted quite a long time without falling prey to pressures for independence from colonial settlers.

In the early days of the Hudson Bay Company, this part of North America was a trading colony, not essentially different from other non-capitalist commercial institutions. Settlement was not a priority and was even a liability to the fur trade, which was the Company's principal concern. After Britain, in the eighteenth century, conquered French territories in America and acquired a large territorial empire in Canada, settlement increased; but it was never entirely clear what purpose the colony served. Geopolitical and military considerations seemed to predominate over economic gains, especially when the colonies to the south gave way to an increasingly powerful independent state and a potential imperial competitor.

Various factors combined to keep the colony in British hands, in part influenced by the disastrous losses south of the border: a disproportionately large military presence in relation to a relatively sparse settler population; the colony's fundamental disunity, dividing not only the English and the French, but the various English-speaking regions, in a colony that for a long time failed to constitute an integrated economy; the large influx of Loyalists from the south during and after the Revolution; and a closer imperial rule, in contrast to the self-governing autonomy enjoyed by the colonies to the south.

The importance of the fur trade in the history of the colony and the long proximity to, and conflict with, the French, to say nothing of the need for support in conflicts with the southern neighbours, also produced a somewhat more accommodating relationship between the colonial power and indigenous peoples than was typical elsewhere in the Empire. In this respect, as in others, Canada was very different from the thirteen colonies that gave birth to the United States and rather less responsive to the logic of the new capitalist imperialism.

The connections between the thirteen colonies and the evolution of capitalism in the imperial homeland are much more obvious. The first major colonies in Virginia and then in Maryland had been based explicitly on the principles of 'improvement' and profit based on production. They were never intended to serve, in the old manner of commercial empires, simply as trading posts. The objective was to develop and exploit the land intensively by cultivating marketable crops and creating industries, on the model of commercial agriculture and textile production at home; and these colonial ventures were regarded as profitable investments, as well as laboratories for domestic projects in England.

The original plan for a diversified commercial economy, however, failed and was soon overtaken by the production of a single, vastly marketable crop, tobacco. This required not only sizeable landholdings and the dispossession of indigenous people but an intensively exploited labour force. At first, this was provided by the 70 or 80 per cent of English immigrants who came to the colonies as indentured servants – the dispossessed and unemployed of England. But as demand for labour increased, while that labour supply became too expensive later in the seventeenth century and eventually dried up as employment opportunities grew in the imperial homeland, there was an increasingly rapid influx of slaves, either directly from Africa or via the Caribbean and its slave plantations. This, of course, gave added impetus to yet another source of commercial profit, the infamous slave trade, which had been going on for some time under the auspices of European empires but now dramatically accelerated. While the colonies had developed in self-conscious imitation of social and economic arrangements in England, and were inserted into a larger increasingly capitalist economy, they developed their own specific mode of commercial exploitation, dominated by a wealthy planter class and worked by slaves.

The growth of slavery in the British colonies is a striking example of how capitalism has, at certain points in its development, appropriated to itself, and even intensified, non-capitalist modes of exploitation. Slavery had never been completely absent from Europe and had made a recovery in the early middle ages, after its sharp decline in the last years of the Roman Empire. As we saw, the Venetians exploited slaves in some of their colonies and supplied slaves to the Arabs. The Portuguese and Spanish empires established the Atlantic slave trade, and the Portuguese in particular pioneered colonial plantation slavery. But, while the British were relative late-comers in the exploitation of slavery, the growth of Britain's capitalist economy gave a new impetus to this old form of exploitation, in the southern

American colonies as well as in the Caribbean. For a time, capitalism even increased the demand for slave labour, as it expanded markets for plantation commodities, at a time when capitalist social property relations made other forms of dependent labour unavailable and a mass free proletariat did not yet exist.

As its domestic economy grew, and as agrarian capitalism opened the way to industrialization, Britain became by far the predominant force in the Atlantic slave trade, even after the American Revolution. After a late start, it seems to have taken hardly more than two decades for Britain to overtake its rivals, the Portuguese and the Dutch. Between 1660 and 1807, when Britain's participation in the carrying of slaves was ended by Parliament, the British apparently 'shipped as many slaves as all other slave-carrying nations put together.'[7] To be sure, Britain's European rivals – and, in the eighteenth century, France in particular – were similarly involved in plantation slavery, especially in sugar production, in which French competition was, for a time, a serious threat to the British. But British development was impelled by the sheer size of Britain's market, swelled by urban industrial classes unlike any others in Europe. There was nothing anywhere else, for example, to match the mass domestic market for sugar that eventually emerged in Britain.

The British colonies, especially in the southern settlements, were also distinguished by the ferocity of the racism they spawned. This was certainly due in large part to the problems of order and control created by the huge and rapid influx of slaves, which were dealt with by means of a stringent legal apparatus that not only severely restricted the freedom of slaves but made slavery a permanent and hereditary condition based on colour. At the same time, as we have seen, the rise of capitalism meant that a wide spectrum of traditional dependent conditions had disappeared, opening a huge chasm between the extremes of legal freedom and chattel slavery. Capitalist development was also accompanied by conceptions of property that encouraged the reduction of slaves to unconditional property, and their complete commodification as chattels. As the dominant forms of labour in the wider capitalist economy were legally free, and at a time when even ideologues of empire like John Locke were declaring that men were by nature free and equal, slaves had to be placed outside the normal universe of natural freedom and equality to justify their permanent subordination. This was accomplished by the construction of more rigid racial categories than had ever existed before – in the form of pseudo-scientific conceptions of race or patriarchal ideologies in which African slaves were perennial children.

The role of slavery in the rise of British capitalism is still a matter of dispute. Some historians have credited profits from the Atlantic slave trade with providing the capital that drove the development of British industrial capitalism.[8] This claim has been challenged by others, who have argued that the profits derived directly from the trade in slaves contributed only a very small proportion of domestic investment in Britain.[9] But it is impossible to deny the importance of the colonies in Britain's highly lucrative external trade, and the essential part played by slaves in producing its highly profitable commodities, tobacco and sugar. Nor can it be denied that industrialization at home, based as it was on the production of cotton textiles, would depend on colonial cotton produced largely by slaves in the West Indies.

The slave plantations of the southern American colonies, then, played a major role in the development of British commerce. In New England and the 'middle' colonies, the intention of colonial administrators was also to establish a profitable commercial agriculture, but here the results were rather different. The New England settlers, who had received their land in the form of townships to be divided by the original 'proprietors', set themselves up as freeholders, while later settlers bought or leased land from them. The original impetus for many of the settlers was to seek refuge from various upheavals at home, the same political, economic and religious turmoil that would produce the English Civil War. In this sense, not having been drawn to the colonies mainly by investors seeking massive profits, they were not so bound to the interests of propertied classes, landlords and merchants at home; and, since their main commercial ties were with the Caribbean colonies, they retained a greater economic independence from the imperial homeland. They did eventually produce a diversified and commercially viable economy, but the objective of most of these settlers was a 'middling' prosperity and household independence.

The middle colonies, in New York, Pennsylvania and New Jersey, established as proprietary colonies, were dominated by large proprietors with closer ties to the imperial power. Typically, the colonial governments granted land to large mercantile companies, which in turn would sell it to large landowners, who leased it to tenant farmers. The elite's imperial connections, however, did not prevent the colonial economy from developing less on the strength of the British domestic market than on the growing interdependence of colonial settlements. The new commercial nexus of landowners and merchants profited greatly from trade with other colonies, producing and marketing basic commodities – such as grain – which were not produced in the southern colonies or the Caribbean, where production was more or less exclusively devoted to the hugely profitable single crops, tobacco and sugar.

Although the colonies enjoyed a remarkable degree of autonomy, the imperial power no doubt envisaged that what direct political rule could not achieve, economic dependency would. For a time, its confidence was not misplaced. While British dominance lasted, the imperial power, and particularly mercantile interests, gained hugely from the commercial opportunities afforded by the colonial economy.

Yet, inevitably, the economic and political connections between colonial America and the imperial power would eventually grow weaker; and, though the colonies were founded on principles derived from English agrarian capitalism, they inevitably developed their own distinctive property relations. At such a great distance, with more or less self-sufficient agriculture and with colonial markets nearer to hand, the colonies were not so easily kept within the economic orbit of the imperial power, and direct political control by the state was even harder to maintain. While the imperial state in the course of the seventeenth century increased its hold on the colonies, direct rule was never a realistic option in the longer term. A colonial economy with a strong foundation of its own, dominated by local elites with their own distinct interests and enjoying substantial degrees of self-government, was bound sooner or later to break the imperial connection.

If the growing capitalist economy in the imperial homeland was insufficiently developed and powerful to exert control by means of economic compulsion, the generation of capitalist imperatives within the colonial economy was not a simple matter either; and the process of capitalist development in the colonies followed a distinctive course. In New England and the middle colonies, '[t]he existence of unoccupied land within easy reach of poor and "middling" settlers undermined the ability of landowners to create a social monopoly of land in the eighteenth century'. At the same time, the hold of urban merchants on much of the land in the interior meant that farmers and artisans often occupied land illegally as squatters. But '[as] long as the colonial militia could not enforce the land speculators' private property rights on the frontier, farmers and rural artisans could establish, maintain and expand their landholding without extensive commodity production.' Tenancy had virtually disappeared by the time of the Revolution, and many independent farmers and artisans whose access to land was not mediated by the market, while they did engage in exchange relations with local and regional merchants, were 'able to reproduce themselves economically without recourse to the market'.[10]

This meant that a large proportion of agricultural producers in the mid-Atlantic region remained for a time outside the orbit of capitalist imperatives. If anything, the economic imperatives emanating from the imperial power were even weaker than before. But ironically, the freedom from capitalist imperatives, as Charles Post has argued, would change radically with the Revolution, as the costs and disruptions of the war, the demands of state governments and the activities of merchants and land speculators, made small and middling farmers increasingly dependent on commodity production simply to maintain their land in the face of growing debt and taxes. They might remain independent commodity producers, but they would be subject to market imperatives. Yet now, of course, the beneficiary of this development was not the imperial power. It was the colonial elites who gained from it. As independent producers became market-dependent for possession of land and their very survival, as they were drawn inexorably into the imperatives of capitalism, there was little to impede the growing political and economic dominance of merchants in the North and planters in the South, or the development of the new state as an imperial power in its own right.

India

That, then, is the background against which the second British Empire took a very different turn – not only because of the very different circumstances in Africa and Asia, and especially in India. The imperial power had learned some lessons from its attempts to establish an empire that depended on the force of economic imperatives as yet neither expansive nor powerful enough to impose themselves successfully on distant colonial economies. The combined effect of these differences was the installation of an empire in India that had more in common with non-capitalist empires than had England's earlier settler colonies in Ireland and America, or even the plantation colonies in the Caribbean.

Beginning as a commercial empire dominated by a monopolistic trading company, British domination gradually took the form of a territorial empire dominated by the imperial state. In both these guises, the empire was essentially non-capitalist in its logic. Yet the transition from one to the other, and the subsequent evolution of British imperial rule, were shaped by Britain's capitalist development.

In the early modern period, when British merchants became seriously interested in trade with Asia, India was at the height of its economic power, with a vast commercial apparatus and great productive capacities, especially in the manufacture of textiles. The English East India Company was an unambiguously non-capitalist institution, which entered into trade in the region in much the same way as other trading companies had done, relying on monopolies, advanced maritime technology and military power to establish commercial advantage over its European rivals. At the same time, neither the Company nor the imperial state were, at first, interested in – or, indeed, capable of – direct territorial rule in India; and there was a general reluctance to overextend imperial rule, which seemed far too dangerous and costly, especially against such a formidable adversary. There was in any case no need for territorial rule, as long as the empire remained a commercial one, and it was likely that the costs it would impose on commerce would outweigh the benefits.

But, by the second half of the eighteenth century, the Company was taking a different approach. It had begun to show less interest in India as a vast commercial opportunity than as a source of revenue, seeking not commercial profits but surpluses extracted directly from producers in the age-old manner of non-capitalist extra-economic exploitation in the form of tax and tribute. The more the attractions of empire as a source of revenue increased, the more the territorial imperative grew. As the empire in India was becoming more, not less, a traditional form of non-capitalist imperialism, based on extra-economic extraction of tribute by way of taxation, it also became more and more a military despotism.

In pursuit of this non-capitalist form of wealth, the Company used its power, economic and military, to establish property relations in India that would ensure a reliable source of revenue. Far from 'modernizing' India, the Company, with the help of the British state, reverted to older, non-capitalist forms. This strategy of 'traditionalizing' Indian society has been blamed for reversing India's economic and social development by entrenching, or even creating, archaic forms of landlord–peasant relations:

> The many members of India's once-great 'military market-place' and erstwhile manufacturing economy, who now were pushed out on to the land, did not become 'traditional' peasants by choice; nor, by doing so, did they challenge the dictates of their colonial masters. Indeed ... in a large number of areas the traditionalization of society appears to have been promoted by

the logic of colonial institutions themselves. It was the Anglo-Hindu lawcourts which enforced the rule of the Brahmanic caste system and disseminated it to deeper social levels. It was the tribunals of the colonial bureaucracy which decreed agrarian society to be based on the self-sufficient village community and the privileges of royalty and aristocracy to be founded on 'ancient' prerogatives held since 'time immemorial'. The assertion of India's Tradition in this context reflected as much an accommodation to the new colonial order as a rejection of it.

... India became a subordinate agricultural colony under the dominance of metropolitan, industrial Britain; its basic cultural institutions were disempowered and 'fixed' in unchanging traditional forms; its 'civil society' was subjected to the suzereignty of a military despotic state.[11]

Just as local landed classes in India depended on extracting surpluses from peasants in the non-capitalist manner, the empire of the East India Company rested on the same foundation. Of course, this meant more and more military adventures, to ensure its territorial base.

The role of the imperial state in these developments was deeply ambiguous. In the early years of the Company's activities in India, the state had largely refrained from interfering in the Company's affairs; but it became increasingly involved in the late eighteenth century, and there was a clear shift in British imperial policy from commercial imperialism to territorial empire. Without the intervention of the British state, the Company could not have secured its predominance in India nor its capacity to transform Indian society. In the process, imperial rule in India became more, rather than less, a traditional kind of militaristic and despotic imperial state, a form of 'military fiscalism', depending on 'traditional' peasants and aristocracies to generate revenue.

But if the involvement of the state was motivated, at least in part, by an effort to gain a share of the revenues extracted by the Company, at the same time, the imperial state clearly felt compelled to intervene precisely because of the Company's non-capitalist strategies and the conviction that they were endangering the empire's commercial value. Critics in the imperial homeland and in the state were concerned that Company policies were interfering with economic gains. Apart from the fact that the state was not particularly successful in getting a share of the revenues, what worried these critics was that the Company was conducting its business on non-commercial principles. So, for instance, Edmund Burke, who was famously critical of the empire in India, headed a parliamentary select committee in 1783 which attacked the Company on the grounds that its economic principles had been 'completely corrupted by turning it into a vehicle for tribute'. It should, they argued, 'fix its commerce upon a commercial basis'.

What it meant to fix commerce upon a commercial basis was also beginning to change. In the early days, the monopoly privileges of the Company made good commercial sense, at least by the standards of non-capitalist commerce. At the same time, anything that could be done to suppress the advantages that India had over domestic industry in Britain because of Indian superiority in textile production was a help to the nascent industry at home. But by the late eighteenth century, there was a growing number of capitalists at home who were more interested in India as a market for their own goods. The Company, and the logic on which it operated, were not keeping up with the development of British capitalism, and the state stepped in.

In this phase of British imperialism, after the era of Robert Clive and Warren Hastings, when the imperial state was asserting its control, there were reforms directed at creating a climate more conducive to commercial profit. These included the establishment of property rights that could resist the extraction of revenue, as well as legal and political reforms intended to transform the state from an instrument of private appropriation into an apparatus of public administration. In other words, without weakening the hold of the imperial power, the intention was to achieve some kind of separation of the economic and political in the capitalist manner.

But there were always contradictory pressures, which drew the imperial state into a non-capitalist logic of rule, into a system of property relations designed to enable the extraction of revenues by Company and state, presided over by an all-embracing military power. The very existence of a territorial empire, and the conditions of its maintenance, generated its own requirements, which often ran counter to commercial imperatives. The pressures were economic, however, no less than political and military. They were not only a response to the inevitable tensions of governing a huge colonial territory, which was always threatening to resist imperial domination, but, paradoxically, also a consequence of Britain's own capitalist development. As British capitalism integrated the international market in such a way as to subject Indian production to the cost/price pressures of capitalist competition, the depression of prices for Indian goods simply aggravated the effects of empire in suppressing Indian industry. This increased the relative attractions of India as a source of revenue directly extracted from the land, rather than a commercial opportunity, and strengthened the imperial motivation for reverting to non-capitalist forms of direct coercive exploitation.

So, while the British state became more and more involved in India as a means of rescuing the empire from the non-capitalist logic imposed on it by the East India Company, it was constantly pulled back to the non-capitalist logic of the Company and the military state. The needs of an empire based on capitalist imperatives were substantially different from those of an empire based on direct military coercion and surplus appropriation by extra-economic means. To be sure, besides the more conventional carnage of military violence, economic imperatives generated their own needs for coercive oppression and gave rise to atrocities such as the large-scale killing and maiming of the Indian workers who constructed the railway. But capitalist imperialism required property forms different from those of a revenue-extracting non-capitalist empire and conditions that would allow market imperatives to regulate the economy. This, on balance, may have been the direction in which the imperial state was trying to move, but conditions in India and the logic of empire itself – not least, the danger of rebellion, culminating in the Mutiny of 1857 – constantly reasserted the primacy of the military state. The evolution of the British Empire would continue to display these contradictory tendencies, oscillating between 'modernization' and 'traditionalization', as the imperatives of capitalism were constantly offset by the logic of an imperial military state, which imposed its own imperatives.

On the face of it, the shift from commercial to territorial empire seems to argue against the proposition that capitalism carries with it a tendency to replace extra-economic with economic forms of exploitation and the expansion of economic imperatives beyond the reach of extra-economic power. Yet, looked at from a different angle, the contradictory development of the British Empire in India is a reflection, not a refutation, of that fundamental premise. The attempt to build a territorial empire on capitalist imperatives was bound to fail, or at least to be plagued by insurmountable contradictions.

How, or even whether, the empire in India was, on balance, profitable to the imperial power, and how, or even whether, it contributed to Britain's economic growth, has long been a matter of heated debate, ever since Adam Smith described it as 'a sort of splendid and showy equipage' that cost more than it was worth. On one side are arguments that British industrialization could not have taken place without commercial profits derived from the empire, and/or without suppressing the Indian economy and its superior textile production. On the other side are arguments which, while not denying that many individuals profited from the empire, or even necessarily that British industrialization gained from it, insist that, in general, the material costs outweighed the benefits. This debate is likely to continue, and there is no intention here of trying to resolve it. But one thing seems indisputable: that the empire in India was a deeply contradictory enterprise.

In an article that spells out in painstaking detail the relative costs and benefits of the empire in India from the mid-nineteenth century, one historian makes an observation that is convincing, whether or not we accept his conclusion that the huge expense of the empire, the increasing costs of governing and preserving it by military force, were unnecessary to the growth of the British economy: 'Only conquests of loot and pillage of the kind maintained by King Leopold in the Congo seem capable of providing metropolitan traders and investors with supernormal profits.'[12] Or, to put it another way, huge profits drawn from extra-economic appropriation are possible only with wholesale and relentless coercion such as King Leopold employed, or at least the coercive extraction practiced by the early Spanish Empire in South America. An empire of constant coercion, violence, looting and pillage may be self-limiting, perhaps because it is too costly to maintain but certainly because sooner or later it destroys the very source of its wealth; but while it lasts, it can yield great profit. By contrast, the profitablitity of *capitalist* imperialism comes into its own only when economic imperatives become strong enough on their own to extend beyond the reach of any conceivable extra-economic power and to impose themselves without day-to-day administration and coercion by an imperial state. The tremendous wealth of India and the huge opportunities it offered for imperialist plunder certainly delayed the day of reckoning; but the British Empire in India clearly, and inevitably, fell between two stools.

Economic imperatives comprehensive and powerful enough to be reliable instruments of imperial domination belong to the twentieth century, and probably only after World War II – in a period that coincides with Indian independence. But this new form of empire would spawn its own contradictions.

6

THE INTERNATIONALIZATION OF CAPITALIST IMPERATIVES

The British Empire carried capitalist imperatives to the farthest corners of the earth, but it did so with limited success and contradictory results. As long as the internationalization of capitalism depended on direct political and military control of subject territories, the demands of colonial rule would inevitably come into conflict with economic imperatives. This is certainly not to say that the development of British capitalism gained nothing from imperial expansion, or even that it lost as much as it gained – though, as we saw in the case of India, we should not confuse the wealth and revenues of empire with the profits of capital or the growth of capitalism. The point is rather that, whatever the contribution of empire to the development of capitalism, that development itself would inevitably break through the limits imposed on it by empire. The growth of capitalism into a universal global power, the globalization of its imperatives, would require a different conduit than simply imperial force.

Britain's European Rivals

The expansion of capitalist imperatives by economic means, rather than by direct imperial domination, began not in colonial territories but much closer to home. Paradoxically, its principal conduit was not colonial coercion but the sovereign nation states of Britain's major European rivals. While Britain subjected its neighbours to its economic imperatives, this did not, of course, have the effect of establishing British hegemony over them. Instead, the major European states mobilized their economies to strengthen their positions in inter-state and inter-imperialist rivalries. Their principal goal was not primarily to challenge Britain in the marketplace by means of competitive production. Economic power may have taken new forms under the influence of British capitalism, but it was pressed into the service of old geopolitical and military objectives.

The development of Britain's rivals, such as Germany and France, was driven by a different mechanism than had propelled the rise of British capitalism. When capitalism emerged in the English country-side, England was certainly part of the European trading system and caught up in the same geopolitical and military rivalries as its neighbours. But it was distinguished by its domestic social property relations, which impelled economic development in specific ways from within; and British industrialization was driven by the impera-tives set in motion by agrarian capitalism. The development of capitalism and industrialization in France and Germany, by contrast, responded to external more than to internal compulsions. The driving force here was not domestic social property relations, impel-ling the capitalist imperatives of competition, capital accumulation and increasing labour productivity, but rather the same geopolitical and military rivalries, and their commercial consequences, that had prevailed in the non-capitalist economies and states of Europe. What had changed was not so much social relations at home in Germany or France as the nature of the external challenge.

War was the principal motivator, as it had been so often before; but British capitalism, and the industrialization that it spawned, had altered the rules of the game. Going into the Napoleonic wars, Britain's head start in industrial development, rooted in the success of agrarian capitalism, gave it a military advantage – perhaps less, at this stage, because of technological superiority than because the economic growth and wealth created by British capitalism could be tapped for military purposes, in ways and degrees unmatched by France.

The Napoleonic empire started from a different material base. At the time of the French Revolution, France was certainly a vibrant and prosperous society, with a flourishing commercial sector. Its technological development may in some respects have even exceeded the British. Yet, despite these advanced technologies, the so-called Industrial Revolution as a social transformation did not originate in France, because the economy was constructed on social property relations that did not impel self-sustaining development, in the way that British capitalism did. English agrarian capitalism gave rise to a productive agriculture worked by a relatively small labour force, creating both an industrial proletariat and a large market for basic consumer goods to supply a population no longer engaged in agricultural production. By contrast, France's agricultural output, although it may have matched the English, was achieved with a still predominantly peasant population and a proportionately larger agrarian labour force. Nor did the Revolution substantially transform French social property relations, and certainly not in a capitalist direction. If anything, it consolidated the position of the peasantry, while the state, and those who held state office, continued to live on peasant-produced surpluses in the form of taxation, as they had in the absolutist age. State office, not capitalist accumulation, was the most highly prized bourgeois career.

When Napoleon came to power, economic activity was certainly facilitated by the removal of internal trade barriers, and by his legal and administrative reforms. But industrial development in the post-Revolutionary period was not impelled by a transformation of class relations, nor even by the growth of a mass market for basic consumer goods, of the kind that had emerged in Britain in the wake of agrarian capitalism. Instead, French industrialization, encouraged by the state, responded to the demands of war, vastly increasing the production of military goods and promoting industries – notably iron and textiles – on which that production depended. Here, class transformations, and the creation of a mass working class, were more result than cause of industrialization.

In the years between the Revolution and the end of the Napoleonic wars, French industrial production, while effective in its particular domain, remained relatively limited in scope; and the agricultural sector, which in Britain had driven economic development, in France remained largely unchanged. The stimulus of war could do much to encourage certain kinds of industrial production, but it could not, by itself, impel the kind of comprehensive and self-sustaining development driven by capitalist imperatives, rooted in the market dependence of producers and appropriators. France did not, and could not at first, respond to the external challenge posed by British capitalism by becoming an essentially competitive economy in an international market. The Napoleonic empire, in fact, supported itself in familiar 'extra-economic' ways, by means of large-scale plunder from its conquered territories, and war was paid for by yet more war; while at home, protected by the state, the French economy, 'turned inward to its peasants, its small-town commerce, and its localized, uncompetitive, and relatively small-scale industries'.[1]

If war encouraged a degree of industrial development, it was only after the defeat of Napoleon, together with the protection afforded by his empire, that the purely economic pressures of British capitalism and the imperatives of competition made themselves felt with full force. France did not respond by trying to reproduce the British pattern of economic development; and, on the face of it, the French economy did not challenge or match British competitive advantages. Whether it could have done so, given its dominant social relations, its peasant majority and the role of the state as a major bourgeois resource, remains an open question. Nor did France keep up with an even later starter, Germany, in industrial development. Yet France did achieve its own economic successes, playing to its strengths and amassing vast capital, investing in certain high value-added domestic industries and in other European economies.

At home, military needs continued to be the main driving force of industrial development, in France as elsewhere in Europe, throughout much of the nineteenth century. The state encouraged not only the production of military equipment but improvements in transport and communication – often with the help of technologies first developed in Britain, to say nothing of British capital. This kind of development, with its characteristic achievements in such industries as iron and steel, and with a high priority given to advances in engineering, would also eventually produce, for instance, the French lead in automobile production – until the car became a mass consumer item, mass-produced by Henry Ford.

The statist tradition in France may seem a weakness by the standards of British capitalism, but it also proved to be a strength. It not only encouraged industrial development in the absence of British-style social property relations, but could also, as the global economy became more competitive, help to administer the restructuring of capital when competitive conditions required it, in a way that a more anarchic and short-termist British capitalism was singularly ill-equipped to do. It should be added that the same tradition has something to do, even today, with the quality of public services in France.

A pattern of state-led economic development, in response to external military pressures, was even more pronounced and successful in Germany. Starting from a far more modest material base, Germany had, by the late nineteenth century, and especially after the creation of a unified state, become an industrial giant and perhaps the most powerful state in Europe. Earlier in the century, at the time of the Napoleonic wars, Germany was a fragmented territory of small principalities, dominated by a conservative aristocracy, while the golden age of German commerce was already in the past. As the philosopher Hegel observed at the time, the German principalities were in no position to confront the massive power of Napoleon. With that inadequacy in mind, Hegel constructed, in his *Philosophy of Right,* a political philosophy based on the premise that what Germany needed to counter such a threat was a French state and a British economy, a synthesis of Napoleon and Adam Smith.

Whether Germany's leaders, especially in Prussia, and later in a unified Germany, were thinking in these philosophical terms, there can be little doubt that the project of state-formation and economic development, which came to fruition under Bismarck in the late nineteenth century, was above all a military enterprise. Its effects were to increase productivity, in agriculture as well as industry, and it was accompanied by substantial innovations in the provision of state and social services. But the pattern of industrial development makes clear the motivating force that drove the German economy. The emblematic case was the giant arms and steel producer, Krupp.

The pattern of German development, even more than the French, presents a striking contrast to the consumer-led industrialization that took place first in Britain. In Britain the evolution of agrarian capitalism had created a mass market for basic consumer goods, at home as well as in the colonies; and the early industrial revolution was launched by relatively small companies producing consumer goods like cotton textiles, with relatively simple technologies and without huge capital investments. The development of the British steel industry, for instance, had as much to do with cutlery as guns. Although this kind of production created its own need for industrial goods, and although Britain did, of course, create its own large corporations engaged in the production of capital goods, the particular origins of British industrial capitalism would continue to shape its economic infrastructure. The nature and size of its enterprises, as well as its commercial culture, differed from the state-led industrialization of Germany, which developed less in pursuit of commercial competitiveness than of military superiority, a pattern that would continue to shape its capitalist development well into the twentieth century.

The Classic Age of Imperialism

The rise of British capitalism, then, certainly had the effect of encouraging industrialization in other major European powers, even without the internal imperatives that drove economic development in Britain. But this did not, at first, have the effect of replacing geopolitical and military rivalries with economic competition. European states in the nineteenth century embarked on even more ferocious campaigns of colonial expansion and conflicts over division of the colonial world, in the classic age of imperialism. This is the historical moment that produced the very idea of imperialism and spawned the major theories designed to analyze it.

The classic theories of imperialism belong to an age when capitalism, while well advanced in parts of the world, was very far from a truly global economic system. Capitalist imperial power certainly did embrace much of the world, but it did so less by the universality of its economic imperatives than by the same coercive force that had always determined relations between colonial masters and subject territories.

Theories of imperialism, especially on the Marxist left, reflected this reality. The major Marxist theorists, like Marx himself, proceeded on the premise that capitalism was still a fairly local phenomenon. Marx had been uncannily prescient in his prediction that capitalism would spread throughout the world. But he was primarily interested in exploring the most mature existing capitalism, industrial Britain; and he explicated the systemic logic of capitalism by examining it as a self-enclosed system, abstracted from the surrounding, largely non-capitalist, world. His major successors had a different starting point. They were mainly interested – for very concrete historical and political reasons – with conditions that, on the whole, were *not* capitalist. These later Marxists generally started from the premise that capitalism would dissolve before it matured, or certainly before it became universal and total. Their main concern was how to navigate within a largely non-capitalist world.

Consider the major milestones in twentieth century Marxist theory. The most famous and influential theories of revolution, from Lenin to Mao, were constructed in situations where capitalism scarcely existed or remained less developed, and where there was no mass proletariat, where the revolution had to depend on alliances between a minority of workers and, in particular, a mass of precapitalist peasants. The classic Marxist theories of imperialism, too, represented an important shift of focus, from the internal operations of advanced capitalist economies to the external relations of capitalism. Major Marxist theorists even in Western Europe became preoccupied with the interactions between capitalism and non-capitalism and the conflicts among capitalist states in relation to the non-capitalist world.

For all the profound disagreements among the classical Marxist theorists of imperialism, they shared one fundamental premise: that imperialism had to do with the location of capitalism in a world that was not – and probably never would be – fully, or even predominantly, capitalist. Underlying the basic Leninist idea that imperialism represented 'the highest stage of capitalism', for instance, was the assumption that capitalism had reached a stage where the main axis of international conflict and military confrontation would run between imperialist states. But that competition was, by definition, rivalry over division and redivision of a largely non-capitalist world. The further capitalism spread (at uneven rates), the more acute would be the rivalry among the main imperialist powers. At the same time, they would face increasing resistance. The whole point – and the reason imperialism was the highest stage of capitalism – was that it was the *final* stage, which meant that capitalism would end before the non-capitalist victims of imperialism were finally and completely swallowed up by capitalism.

The point is made most explicitly by Rosa Luxemburg. The essence of her classic work in political economy, *The Accumulation of Capital*, is to offer an alternative, or supplement, to Marx's analysis of capitalism – essentially in one country – as a self-enclosed system. Her argument is that the capitalist system needs an outlet in non-capitalist formations, which is why capitalism inevitably means militarism and imperialism. Capitalist militarism, having gone through various stages beginning with the straightforward conquest of territory, has now reached its 'final' stage, as 'a weapon in the competitive struggle between capitalist countries for areas of non-capitalist civilization'. But one of the fundamental contradictions of capitalism, she suggests, is that '[a]lthough it strives to become universal, and, indeed, on account of this tendency, it must break down – because it is immanently incapable of becoming a universal form of production.' It is the first mode of economy that tends to engulf the whole world, but it is also the first that cannot exist by itself because it 'needs other economic systems as a medium and soil'.[2]

So in these theories of imperialism, capitalism by definition assumes a non-capitalist environment. In fact, capitalism depends for its survival not only on the existence of these non-capitalist formations but on essentially precapitalist instruments of 'extra-economic' force, military and geopolitical coercion, and on traditional inter-state rivalries, colonial wars and territorial domination. These accounts were profoundly illuminating about the age in which they were written; and, to this day, it has still not been demonstrated they were wrong in assuming that capitalism could not universalize its successes and the prosperity of the most advanced economies, nor that the major capitalist powers would always depend on exploiting subordinate economies. But we have yet to see a systematic theory of imperialism designed for a world in which all international relations are internal to capitalism and governed by capitalist imperatives. That, at least in part, is because a world of more or less universal capitalism, in which capitalist imperatives are a universal instrument of imperial domination, is a very recent development.

Europe, however advanced the development of capitalism may have been in parts of it, went into World War I as a continent of rival geopolitical and military empires. The United States, too, played its part in this old imperial system. Since the early days of the

Monroe Doctrine, it had extended its 'sphere of influence', in the Western hemisphere and beyond, by military means, if not (or not always) for the purpose of direct colonization, then certainly to ensure compliant regimes.

The world emerged from the war with some of the major imperial powers in shreds. But if the classic age of imperialism effectively ended in 1918, and if the US was already showing signs of becoming the world's first truly economic empire (not, of course, without a great deal of extra-economic force on its side and a history of direct imperial violence), several more decades would pass before a new form of empire clearly emerged. It can, in fact, hardly be said to have happened before the end of World War II.

The latter may have been the last major war among capitalist powers to be driven by a quest for outright territorial expansion in pursuit of economic goals – above all, Germany's campaign, launched in compliance with its major industrial interests, for control not only of Eastern European land and resources but even of Caspian and Caucasian oil fields. It was also perhaps the last conflict among capitalist powers in which, while pursuing economic interests, the principal aggressors relied completely on extra-economic force rather than market imperatives, subjecting their own economies to total control by thoroughly militarized states. When the two defeated powers, Germany and Japan, emerged as the principal economic competitors to the US economy, with a great deal of help from the victors, a new age had truly begun.

This would be an age in which economic competition – in uneasy tandem with the cooperation among capitalist states required to guarantee their markets – overtook military rivalry among the major capitalist powers. The main axis of military and geopolitical conflict would run not between capitalist powers but between the capitalist and the developed non-capitalist world – until the Cold War ended with even the former Soviet Union drawn into the capitalist orbit. Yet, if this conflict was not between rival capitalist powers, it certainly had wide-ranging implications for the global capitalist order.

The conflict between the US and USSR never issued in direct military confrontation, yet the Cold War marked a major transition in the role of imperial military power. Without seeking outright territorial expansion, the US nevertheless became the world's most powerful military force, with a highly militarized economy. It was during this time that the purpose of military power shifted decisively away from the relatively well defined goals of imperial expansion and interimperialist rivalry to the open-ended objective of policing the world in the interests of (US) capital. This military pattern, and the needs that it served, would not change with the 'collapse of Communism'; and the Cold War would be replaced by other scenarios of war without end. Today's Bush Doctrine is directly descended from strategies born in the Cold War.

Relations with the less developed world were altered too. In the wake of World War I, as empires crumbled, nation states proliferated. This was not only a consequence of national liberation struggles but also, typically, a matter of imperialist policy. In the Middle East, for example, Western powers, notably Britain and France, began to carve up the remnants of the Ottoman Empire, not by appropriating them as direct colonial possessions but by creating new and somewhat arbitrary states, to suit their own imperial purposes, mainly to control the oil supply – a task later taken over by the United States.

The new imperialism that would eventually emerge from the wreckage of the old would no longer be a relationship between imperial masters and colonial subjects but a complex interaction between more-or-less sovereign states. This capitalist imperialism certainly absorbed the world into its economic orbit, but it was increasingly a world of nation states. The US emerged from World

War II as the strongest economic and military power, and took command of a new imperialism governed by economic imperatives and administered by a system of multiple states – with all the contradictions and dangers this combination would present. This economic empire would be sustained by political and military hegemony over a complex state system, consisting of enemies who had to be contained, friends who had to be kept under control, and a 'third world' that had to be made available to western capital.

Globalization

As this book was being written, a new nation state was born. After a long, bitter and courageous struggle, East Timor had won its independence from Indonesia. The history of this new state encapsulates the development of imperialism, from its non-capitalist origins to capitalist 'globalization': colonization of Timor by Portugal in the sixteenth century, for the usual reasons, such as access to resources and slave labour; conflict between Portuguese and Dutch colonial interests, ultimately leading to division of the island between the imperial powers in the nineteenth century, with the east remaining in Portuguese hands; the replacement of direct European colonization in the late twentieth century by a local dictator, Indonesia's Suharto, who was useful to the West and supported by Western states, particularly the US, in his murderous oppression of East Timor; and finally, an independent nation state, won by bloody struggle and already, even while still in gestation, subject to new pressures from the West.

It remains to be seen how imperial power will impose its imperatives on the tiny new state. But the very conditions that should make it capable of some independence from those imperatives, and free of the debt which is the principal instrument of the new imperialism, are the very ones that make it vulnerable to imperial pressures: large oil and gas reserves, under the sea between the island and Australia. We can be sure that Australia, with the help of the US, will do all it can to ensure the most favourable conditions for the big oil companies and imperial economies; and the likelihood of East Timor remaining free of debt must be very much in question.

As East Timor was emerging into statehood, the UN set out to negotiate on its behalf a new energy treaty, to extract better terms than Indonesia had obtained years before from Australia and the major oil companies. The US government, in the person of Vice-President Dick Cheney, an oilman himself, stepped in to warn against going too far. This is only a hint of things to come, as East Timor finds itself forced to navigate in a world dominated by the massive economic and military power of the US. The new Timorese government has already been forced, by a threat from Colin Powell to withhold US aid, to give a written promise not to prosecute US citizens for crimes against humanity in the international criminal court.[3]

East Timor is only the latest example, on a very small scale, of the new imperialism's preferred strategy. The current imperial hegemon has been able, increasingly since World War II, and certainly since the collapse of Communism, to dictate its conditions to the world, not without military coercion but certainly without direct colonial rule. It has found various ways of imposing its economic imperatives on ostensibly independent states.

The formal beginning of this new imperial order can be dated quite precisely, during and immediately after the war. The US asserted its military supremacy with its atom bombs in Hiroshima and Nagasaki, and its economic hegemony with the establishment of the Bretton Woods system, the IMF, the World Bank and, somewhat later, the General Agreement on Tariffs and Trade (GATT). The ostensible purpose of these agreements and institutions was to stabilize the world economy, rationalize its currencies by making them freely convertible against the US dollar, and establish a framework for economic reconstruction and development. But these objectives were to be achieved on very particular terms. The goal was to open other economies, their resources, their labour and their markets, to western, and especially US, capital. This was to be accomplished by the simple means of making the reconstruction of European economies and the development of the 'third world' dependent on their compliance with conditions imposed in the main by the US. These global economic institutions were accompanied by a political organization, the United Nations. Designed to have little effect on the global economy, the UN would play a part in maintaining some semblance of political order in a system of multiple states, its very existence discouraging forms of international organization less congenial to the dominant powers.

At this stage, with a booming economy in the US, the imperial power was interested in encouraging a kind of 'development' and 'modernization' in the third world, as a means of expanding its own markets. When the long postwar boom ended, its requirements changed, and the objective of expanding markets was overtaken by other needs. While the general purpose of the postwar economic order, up to and including – or especially – the recent phase of 'globalization', has remained essentially the same, the specific rules of the world economy have been transformed, in keeping with the changing needs of US capital. The Bretton Woods system was abandoned in the early 1970s, to be replaced by other principles of economic order, in accordance with changing imperial needs.

This was the beginning of the long downturn, which affected all western economies, and the US in particular, until the early nineties (indeed, even till today, although its consequences have been masked by the stock market bubble and the 'wealth effect'). The global economy was made to carry the burden of that decline. After the heady decades of sustained growth and increasing productivity during the long boom, the US economy entered a long period of stagnation and declining profitability, a characteristically – and uniquely – capitalist crisis of overcapacity and overproduction, not least because its former military adversaries, Japan and Germany, had become extremely effective economic competitors. The problem now was how to displace the crisis, in space and in time.[4]

What followed was the period we call globalization, the internationalization of capital, its free and rapid movements and the most predatory financial speculation around the globe. This was, as much as anything else, a response not to the successes but to the failures of capitalism. The US used its control of financial and commercial networks to postpone the day of reckoning for its own domestic capital, enabling it to shift the burden elsewhere, easing the movements of excess capital to seek profits wherever they were to be found, in an orgy of financial speculation.

Conditions were imposed on developing economies to suit these new needs. In what came to be called the 'Washington Consensus', and through the medium of the IMF and the World Bank, the imperial power demanded 'structural adjustment' and a variety of measures which would have the effect of making these economies even more vulnerable to the pressures of US-led global capital: for instance, an emphasis on production for export and the removal of import controls, which made producers market-dependent for their own survival, while opening them, especially in the case of agricultural production, to competition from highly subsidized western producers; the privatization of public services, which would then become vulnerable to takeover by companies based in the major capitalist powers; high interest rates and financial deregulation, which produced vast gains for US financial interests, while creating a debt crisis in the third world (and ultimately, in one of the perennial contradictions of capitalism, a recession at home in the imperial centre); and so on.

That, of course, is not the end of the story, but this is not the place to explore the boom and bust cycles of capitalism or its tendencies to long-term downturn and stagnation. It suffices to say that the kind of control of the global economy enjoyed by the US, while it cannot resolve the contradictions of the 'market economy', can be used, and is being used, to compel other economies to serve the interests of the imperial hegemon in response to the fluctuating needs of its own domestic capital – by manipulating debt, the rules of trade, foreign aid and the whole financial system. One minute, it can force subsistence farmers to shift to single cash-crop production for export markets; the next, according to need, it can effectively wipe out those farmers by demanding the opening of third world markets, while protecting and subsidizing its own agricultural producers. It can temporarily support industrial production in emerging economies by means of financial speculation; and then suddenly pull the rug out from under those economies by cashing in the speculative profits, or cutting losses and moving on. The fact that, sooner or later, the effects of these practices will come back to haunt the imperial economy is only one of the many contradictions of this imperial system.

Actually existing globalization, then, means the opening of subordinate economies and their vulnerability to imperial capital, while the imperial economy remains sheltered as much as possible from the obverse effects. Globalization has nothing to do with free trade. On the contrary, it is about the careful control of trading conditions, in the interests of imperial capital. To argue, as some commentators do, that the problem with globalization is not that there is too much of it but that there is not enough, that what poor countries need is truly free trade and access to western markets, is to miss the point of globalization in a fundamental way. If the openness of the global economy were a two-way street, whatever else that might achieve, it would not serve the purpose for which the system was designed; and, in any case, the principal danger to the poor economies is less the closure of imperial markets than the vulnerability of their own to imperial capital.

Let us be clear about what globalization is and, more particularly, what it is not. It is not, to begin with, a truly integrated world economy. No one can doubt that movements of capital across national boundaries are frequent and breathtakingly rapid in today's global economy, or that new supranational institutions have emerged to facilitate those movements. But whether that means that markets are substantially more globally integrated than ever before is another question.

The first and most elementary point is that so-called 'transnational' corporations generally have a base, together with dominant shareholders and boards, in single nation states and depend on them in many fundamental ways. Beyond that, some commentators have argued that, according to various measures of integration, globalization is far from advanced, and in important respects is less so than in previous eras – for instance, in the magnitude of international trade as a share of gross domestic product, or global exports as a proportion of the global product.

But let us accept that the speed and extent of capital movements, especially those that depend on new information and communication technologies, have created something new. Let us even accept that the world is more 'interdependent', at least in the sense that the effects of economic movements in the heartlands of capital are felt throughout the globe. There remains one overriding indication that the global market is still far from integrated: the fact that wages, prices and conditions of labour are still so widely diverse throughout the world. In a truly integrated market, market imperatives would impose themselves universally, to compel all competitors to approximate some common social average of labour productivity and costs, in order to survive in conditions of price competition.

This apparent failure of global integration is not, however, a failure of globalization so much as a symptom of it. Globalization has been as much about *preventing* as promoting integration. The global movements of capital require not only free transborder access to labour, resources and markets but also protection from the opposite movements, as well as a kind of economic and social fragmentation that enhances profitability by differentiating the costs and conditions of production. Here again, it is the nation state that must perform the delicate balancing act between opening borders to global capital and deterring a kind and degree of integration that might go too far in levelling social conditions among workers throughout the world.

It cannot even be said unequivocally that global capital would gain most from levelling the costs of labour downward by subjecting workers'in advanced capitalist countries to the competition of low-cost labour regimes. This is certainly true, up to a point. But, apart from the dangers of social upheaval at home, there is the inevitable contradiction between capital's constant need to drive down the costs of labour and its constant need to expand consumption, which requires that people have money to spend. This, too, is one of the insoluble contradictions of capitalism. But, on balance, global capital benefits from uneven development, at least in the short term (and short-termism is an endemic disease of capitalism). The fragmentation of the world into separate economies, each with its own social regime and labour conditions, presided over by more or less sovereign territorial states, is no less essential to 'globalization' than is the free movement of capital. Not the least important function of the nation state in globalization is to enforce the principle of nationality that makes it possible to manage the movements of labour by means of strict border controls and stringent immigration policies, in the interests of capital.

The Indispensable State

Some of the best-known critics of globalization, at least in the dominant capitalist economies, characterize it mainly as a development driven and dominated by transnational corporations, whose infamous brand names – Nike, McDonald's, Monsanto, and so on – are the symbols of today's global capitalism. At the same time, they seem to assume that the services traditionally performed by the nation state for national capital must now be performed for transnational corporations by some kind of global state. In the absence of such a state, the political work of global capital is apparently being done by transnational institutions such as the WTO, the IMF, the World Bank or the G8. Anti-capitalist movements acting on these assumptions have targetted transnational corporations by such means as consumer boycotts, sabotage and demonstrations; and they have directed their oppositional energies against supranational organizations which appear to be the institutions that come closest to representing the political arm of global capital, in the way that the nation state has traditionally represented national capital.

These 'anti-capitalist' movements have been effective in bringing to light the devastating effects of 'globalization', especially in capturing the attention of the advanced capitalist world, which has long ignored the consequences of global capitalism. They have raised the consciousness of many people throughout the world, and they have offered the promise of new oppositional forces. But it may be that in some respects they are based on faulty premises. The conviction that global corporations are the ultimate source of globalization's evils, and that the power of global capital is politically represented above all in supranational institutions like the WTO, may be based on the assumption that global capitalism behaves the way it does because it is global, rather than (or more than) because it is capitalist. The principal task for oppositional forces, it seems, is to target the instruments of capital's global reach rather than to challenge the capitalist system itself.

In fact, many participants in movements of this kind are not so much anti-capitalist as anti-'globalization', or perhaps anti-neoliberal, or even just opposed to particularly malignant corporations. They assume that the detrimental effects of the capitalist system can be eliminated by taming global corporations or by making them more 'ethical', 'responsible', and socially conscious.

But even those who are more inclined to oppose the capitalist system itself may assume that the more global the capitalist economy becomes, the more global the political organization of capital will be. So, if globalization has made the national state increasingly irrelevant, anti-capitalist struggles must move immediately beyond the nation state, to the global institutions where the power of global capital truly lies.

We need to examine these assumptions critically, but not because anti-capitalist movements are wrong in their conviction that transnational corporations are doing great damage and need to be challenged, or that the WTO and the IMF are doing the work of global capital – which is certainly true. Nor are these movements wrong in their internationalism or their insistence on solidarity among oppositional forces throughout the world. We need to scrutinize the relation between global capital and national states because even the effectiveness of international solidarity depends on an accurate assessment of the forces available to capital and those accessible to opposition.

It should be clear by now that, just as globalization is not a truly integrated world economy, it is also not a system of declining nation states. On the contrary, the state lies at the very heart of the new global system. As we saw in Chapter 1, the state continues to play its essential role in creating and maintaining the conditions of capital accumulation; and no other institution, no transnational agency, has even begun to replace the nation state as an administrative and coercive guarantor of social order, property relations, stability or contractual predictability, or any of the other basic conditions required by capital in its everyday life.

Just as the state is far from powerless, multinational corporations are far from all-powerful. Scrutiny of corporate operations is likely to reveal that 'multinational enterprises are not particularly good at managing their international operations', and that profits tend to be lower, while costs are higher, than in domestic operations.[5] These enterprises 'have very little control over their own international operations, let alone over globalisation'. Any success such companies have had in the global economy has depended on the indispensable support of the state, both in the locale of their home base and elsewhere in their 'multinational' network.

The state, in both imperial and subordinate economies, still provides the indispensable conditions of accumulation for global capital, no less than for very local enterprises; and it is, in the final analysis, the state that has created the conditions enabling global capital to survive and to navigate the world. It would not be too much to say that the state is the *only* non-economic institution truly indispensable to capital. While we can imagine capital continuing its daily operations if the WTO were destroyed, and perhaps even welcoming the removal of obstacles placed in its way by organizations that give subordinate economies some voice, it is inconceivable that those operations would long survive the destruction of the local state.

Globalization has certainly been marked by a withdrawal of the state from its social welfare and ameliorative functions; and, for many observers, this has perhaps more than anything else created an impression of the state's decline. But, for all the attacks on the welfare state launched by successive neoliberal governments, it cannot even be argued that global capital has been able to dispense with the social functions performed by nation states since the early days of capitalism. Even while labour movements and forces on the left have been in retreat, with so-called social democratic governments joining in the neoliberal assault, at least a minimal 'safety net' of social provision has proved to be an essential condition of economic success and social stability in advanced capitalist countries. At the same time, developing countries that may in the past have been able to rely more on traditional supports, such as extended families and village communities, have been under pressure to shift at least some of these functions to the state, as the process of 'development' and the commodification of life have destroyed or weakened old social networks – though, ironically, this has made them even more vulnerable to the demands of imperial capital, as privatization of public services has become a condition of investment, loans and aid.

Oppositional movements must struggle constantly to maintain anything close to decent social provision. But it is hard to see how any capitalist economy can long survive, let alone prosper, without a state that to some extent, however inadequately, balances the economic and social disruptions caused by the capitalist market and class exploitation. Globalization, which has further undermined traditional communities and social networks, has, if anything, made this state function more rather than less necessary to the preservation of the capitalist system. This does not mean that capital will ever willingly encourage social provision. It simply means that its hostility to social programmes, as being necessarily a drag on capital accumulation, is one of capitalism's many insoluble contradictions.

On the international plane, too, the state continues to be vital. The new imperialism, in contrast to older forms of colonial empire, depends more than ever on a system of multiple and more or less sovereign national states. The very fact that 'globalization' has extended capital's purely economic powers far beyond the range of any single nation state means that global capital requires *many* nation states to perform the administrative and coercive functions that sustain the system of property and provide the kind of day-to-day regularity, predictability, and legal order that capitalism needs more than any other social form. No conceivable form of 'global governance' could provide the kind of daily order or the conditions of accumulation that capital requires.

The world today is more than ever a world of nation states. The political form of globalization is not a global state or global sovereignty. Nor does the lack of correspondence between global economy and national states simply represent some kind of time-lag in political development. The very essence of globalization is a global economy administered by a global system of multiple states and local sovereignties, structured in a complex relation of domination and subordination.

The administration and enforcement of the new imperialism by a system of multiple states has, of course, created many problems of its own. It is not a simple matter to maintain the right kind of order among so many national entities, each with its own internal needs and pressures, to say nothing of its own coercive powers. Inevitably, to manage such a system ultimately requires a single overwhelming military power, which can keep all the others in line. At the same time, that power cannot be allowed to disrupt the orderly predictability that capital requires, nor can war be allowed to endanger vital markets and sources of capital. This is the conundrum that confronts the world's only superpower.

'SURPLUS IMPERIALISM', WAR WITHOUT END

For the first time in the history of the modern nation state, the world's major powers are not engaged in direct geopolitical and military rivalry. Such rivalry has been effectively displaced by competition in the capitalist manner. Yet, the more economic competition has overtaken military conflict in relations among major states, the more the US has striven to become the most overwhelmingly dominant military power the world has ever seen.

Why is it necessary, in the new capitalist world order, for the US to account for at least 40 per cent of the world's military spending, particularly when it has so many unfulfilled needs at home – not least, for instance, the need for a decent health care system? Why is there such an unprecedented disparity of power in the world, in which the most significant 'asymmetry' is not between the US and 'rogue states' or 'terrorists' but 'between the US and the rest of the powers'?[1] It has been said that the US now possesses a military force greater than the next eight powers put together (and by some measures, greater than *all* other countries combined), while its budget is equal to the next twelve to fifteen combined. Some might call this 'surplus imperialism', but whatever its name, the reasons for it are not at all obvious.[2]

That is the paradox of the new imperialism. It is the first imperialism in which military power is designed neither to conquer territory nor even to defeat rivals. It is an imperialism that seeks no territorial expansion or physical dominance of trade routes. Yet it has produced this enormous and disproportionate military capability, with an unprecedented global reach. It may be precisely because the new imperialism has no clear and finite objectives that it requires such massive military force. Boundless domination of a global economy, and of the multiple states that administer it, requires military action without end, in purpose or time.

War Without End

When, in 2001, the US (and Britain) failed to launch a massive attack on Afghanistan within days of the September 11 atrocities, there was almost universal surprise, whether tinged with disappointment or relief.[3] People had come to expect, as a matter of course, an immediate and massive high-tech assault, which would spare the lives and limbs of US forces while inflicting much 'collateral damage'. But this time, we were told, the White House 'moderates' had won, at least for a time, if only because the exigencies of preserving the coalition against terrorism counselled caution, or because winter was too near, or because the Taliban might simply implode without a fight. Any attack – and there might be none at all – would be 'measured' and 'proportionate'. Optimists hoped that Bush had learned the virtues of multilateralism. Pessimists feared the worst was still to come. But critics and supporters were united in their wonder at the temperance displayed by the world's only superpower.

Then the bombing started. The massive high-tech assault, with all the collateral damage, proceeded as before. Still, hopes were voiced that the strikes would be carefully targetted and 'proportionate' and that the campaign would be short. In the meantime, the US told the UN that it reserved the right to keep its options open for possible strikes on targets other than Afghanistan. As the Taliban regime in Afghanistan collapsed, the end of the 'war against terrorism' was even further away than it seemed at the start.

Some of the reasoning behind this open-ended military project was revealed at the beginning of the war. On 30 September, the *Observer* in London carried a special report, 'Inside the Pentagon':

> As war begins in Afghanistan, so does the assault on the White House – to win the ear and signed orders of the military's Commander in Chief, President George W. Bush, for what Pentagon hawks call 'Operation Infinite War'. . . .
>
> The Observer has learnt that two detailed proposals for warfare without limit were presented to the President this week by his Defense Secretary Donald Rumsfeld, both of which were temporarily put aside but remain on hold. They were drawn up by his deputy, Paul Wolfowitz. . . . The plans argue for open-ended war without constraint either of time or geography. . . .
>
> [T]he Pentagon militants prefer to speak of 'revolving alliances', which look like a Venn diagram, with an overlapping centre and only certain countries coming within the US orbit for different sectors and periods of an unending war. The only countries in the middle of the diagrammatic rose, where all the circles overlap, are the US, Britain and Turkey.
>
> Officials say that in a war without precedent, the rules have to be made up as it develops, and that the so-called 'Powell Doctrine' arguing that there should be no military intervention without 'clear and achievable' political goals is 'irrelevant'. . . .[4]

The repudiation of the notion that military intervention must have clear and achievable political goals speaks volumes, and it articulates a doctrine that has developed since the Cold War. The US and its allies, notably Britain, have been redefining war and the criteria by which we judge it. The new doctrine of war that seems to be emerging is a necessary corollary to a new form of empire.

Immediately after the September 11 atrocities, President Bush announced that his purpose was to rid the world of evil-doers. At that moment, the 'war against terrorism' was being called 'Operation Infinite Justice'. Some time later, Prime Minister Blair told the Labour Party Conference that the present campaign should be part of a larger project of 'reordering our world'. Nothing that was said before or after did much either to clarify or to narrow these grandiose ambitions. Sympathetic observers were no less at a loss than critics to explain precisely what the objective of the first military round would be: to capture Osama bin Laden; to destroy al-Qaeda's training camps (by then surely empty); or to overthrow the Taliban, with or without installing a new government; to say nothing of further objectives, such as attacks on Iraq to complete the job left unfinished by former president George Bush Senior.

In the face of these uncertainties, there was a tendency to assume either that the White House was simply divided between hawks and doves, or that the administration was simply confused, with no real idea what to do. And there was a strong temptation to dismiss Blair's delusions of grandeur as a means of deflecting scrutiny from his failures at home. No doubt there is something to be said for all these interpretations. But we need to take more seriously the significance of Bush and Blair's grand design.

There is, of course, nothing new about the United States resorting to military action to pursue its imperial interests and sustain its economic hegemony. It should hardly need saying that, since World

War II, the US has engaged in one military venture after another. There exists a convention among some commentators that the US has been a remarkably reluctant global power, disinclined to use its military force. But, while it is certainly true that the US is averse to taking casualties among its own forces, this has not prevented regular military interventions, including not only major wars in Korea and Vietnam but also repeated smaller incursions into other parts of the world, from Central America to Africa. Nonetheless, something new has been emerging, especially since the end of the Cold War. If we discount the overblown self-righteous rhetoric from George W. Bush and Tony Blair, there remains a new military doctrine, which, while making the most extravagant moral claims, nonetheless departs from centuries of discourse on 'just war'.

The just war tradition has always been notoriously elastic and infinitely capable of adjustment to the varying interests of dominant classes, encompassing everything up to and including the most aggressive and predatory imperial adventures. Throughout the changing character of war and imperialism, ideologies of justification have been able to remain within certain conceptual limits and to operate with certain basic principles. Even 'positivist' conceptions of international law, which recognize no principles of justice emanating from a higher, divine authority, have subscribed to certain basic tenets associated with 'just war'. The new doctrine, while invoking the traditions of just war, has for the first time in centuries found those principles insufficiently flexible and has effectively discarded them. Just as earlier adjustments were made to fit changing contexts and requirements, the current rupture also has its specific historical context and bespeaks particular imperial needs.

The doctrine of 'just war', throughout its permutations, enunciates a few essential requirements for going to war: there must be a just cause; war must be declared by a proper authority, with the right intention, and after other means have been exhausted; there must be a reasonable chance of achieving the desired end, and the means must be proportionate to that end. We have already encountered some of the ingenious ways in which those apparently stringent requirements have been made compatible with the most aggressive wars of commercial rivalry and imperial expansion. The doctrine has often been stretched to its limits and rendered effectively meaningless – by Hugo Grotius, for instance, who found a way of justifying, among other things, the use of military force by private trading companies. But the current doctrine breaks with the tradition of European military theory and practice in wholly new ways.

Every US war claims a just cause, a proper authority and right intentions, while insisting that there is no other way. Those claims are, of course, more than a little debatable. But at least these justifications of US military campaigns, however contestable they may be, up to this point remain within the limits of just war argumentation. The rupture occurs most clearly in the other two conditions: that there must be a reasonable chance of achieving the goals of any military action, and that the means must be proportionate.

There are two senses in which the new doctrine of war, most recently enunciated by Bush and Blair, violates the first of these two principles. It is, needless to say, clear that no military action could possibly rid the world of Bush's 'evil-doers'. For that matter, the 'war against terrorism' can hardly be said to have a reasonable chance of ending terrorism. If anything, it stands a better chance of aggravating terrorist violence. Nor can military action, with or without humanitarian admixtures, reorder the world in the way outlined by Blair.

But it is just as clear that the new doctrine departs from the principle of achievable goals in ways inconceivable to any earlier proponents of the just war doctrine. This particular principle was directed against futile and self-destructive adventures by forces lacking the means to achieve their ends and more likely to make their own conditions worse. The present case has to do with the world's most powerful military force, the most powerful the world has ever known, which could confidently expect to achieve any reasonable military goal. So a new principle is being established here: it could simply mean that military action can after all be justified without any hope of achieving its aim, but it would probably be more accurate to say that military action now requires no specific aim at all.

Such a principle naturally affects the means–ends calculus too. We are accustomed to criticizing the US and its allies for undertaking actions which in their massively destructive means are unsuited to their professed ends. But we may now be compelled to discard the principle of proportionality altogether – not simply because we are being asked to accept 'disproportionate' means but because, in the absence of specific ends, no such calculus is relevant at all. There is a new principle of war *without end*, either in purpose or in time.

The 'war against terrorism' is not the first instance of the new doctrine. It certainly has roots in the Cold War. Even the 'war on drugs', insofar as it undoubtedly has a military component (whether directly conducted by the US or, with its assistance, by, say, Colombian forces), has had something of this flavour. But another important step in establishing the new doctrine has been the notion of 'humanitarian war'. It is certainly in this connection that the constraints of old just war principles were first most explicitly discarded.

It is by now a well-known story that, in their dispute over war in the Balkans, the former US Secretary of State, Madeleine Albright, then Ambassador to the UN, challenged the current Secretary of State, Colin Powell, then head of the Joint Chiefs of Staff, over his objection to military intervention in Bosnia. Underlying his objection was the so-called 'Powell Doctrine', a military doctrine in the old just war tradition, requiring that military action have clear and finite ends, adequate means, and exit strategies. 'What's the point of having this superb military that you've always been talking about,' Albright angrily protested, 'if we can't use it?' What Albright was challenging was certainly not a doctrine opposed to any military action ever. Powell, as a military man, was hardly advocating pacifism. Where they parted company was precisely at the point that traditional doctrines of just war require specific and finite achievable ends and commensurate means.

But if Madeleine Albright represents a milestone in the development of this new doctrine, it has long been a pattern for political figures in the US to depart from the old one. When Henry Kissinger advocated the unpredictable use of military force, he, like Albright, had in mind the use of force for political purposes far more diffuse and inchoate than the achievement of some specific military goal, as did others throughout the Cold War. To be sure, he was not particularly given to just war arguments and was generally quite open about his adherence to the apparently opposing principles of amoral *raison d'état*. But other political leaders, in support of the same policies, have had no difficulty invoking the justice of war. Today, when Colin Powell himself is Secretary of State, he is being challenged by non-military politicians such as Donald Rumsfeld, Paul Wolfowitz, and Dick Cheney, together with Bush advisers such as Richard Perle, whose views are even more clearly antithetical to the old just war principles of ends and means. Their plan, 'Operation Infinite War', calls for an open-ended war with no limits of time or geography.

President Bush has recently enunciated a new military doctrine, which amounts to an open-ended declaration of perpetual war. In a new policy of 'defensive intervention', which breaks with long-standing military doctrines of containment and deterrence, the US now claims the right to undertake massive preemptive strikes, wherever and whenever it feels so inclined, not for any clearly definable reason, and certainly not only in the face of an existing military threat, but merely in anticipation of some future danger – or even none at all. The Bush administration has since made it unambiguously clear that the doctrine of preemptive strikes includes the use of nuclear weapons. This endless state of war is also supported by a new political and ideological climate, ranging from the erosion of civil liberties to the discouragement, even the suppression, of dissent.[5]

There are 'no stages', says Richard Perle, in the 'war on terrorism':

> This is total war. We are fighting a variety of enemies. There are lots of them out there. All this talk about first we are going to do Afghanistan, then we will do Iraq, then we take a look around and see how things stand. This is entirely the wrong way to go about it. . . . If we just let our vision of the world go forth, and embrace it entirely, and we don't try to piece together clever diplomacy, but just wage a total war . . . our children will sing great songs about us years from now.[6]

So there we have it: total and infinite war – not necessarily continuous war but war indefinite in its duration, objectives, means and spatial reach.

Universal Capitalism

The new ideology of war without end answers to the particular needs of the new imperialism. This imperialism, which emerged only in the twentieth century, or even only after World War II, belongs to a capitalist world. It may seem odd to situate this capitalist world so late in history, and even so late in the development of capitalism itself. But recent decades have been distinguished by the *universality* of capitalism, and even when the USSR still existed, the imperatives of capitalism left their mark on the whole world. The Marxist theories of imperialism, as we saw in the previous chapter, belonged to a different imperialist age, in which it could not be assumed, even so late in the development of capitalism, that the latter would ever be as universal as it is today.

But if capitalist imperatives now span the world, they have not displaced the territorial state. On the contrary, the more universal capitalism has become, the more it has needed an equally universal system of reliable local states. Nonetheless, just as we have not yet seen a systematic theory of imperialism in a world of universal capitalism, we have no theory of imperialism that adequately comprehends a world that consists not of imperial masters and colonial subjects but of an international system in which both imperial and subordinate powers are more or less sovereign states.

We may be hearing more today about imperialism than we have for a long time, and theories of globalization as a form of imperialism are not in short supply. But to characterize globalization in the conventional way, as the decline of the territorial state, is to miss what may be most novel and distinctive about the new imperialism, its unique mode of economic domination managed by a system of multiple states. The specificities of this imperialist mode are only now beginning to emerge; and, more particularly, the specific role played by military force in this new context is only now finding expression in a systematic ideology of war.

In the earliest days of capitalist imperialism there emerged, in rudimentary form, a conception of empire not as conquest or even military domination and political jurisdiction, but as purely economic hegemony. John Locke, as we saw, best reflected this new conception. His theory of colonial appropriation bypassed the question of political jurisdiction or the right of one political power to dominate another; and in his theory of property, we can observe imperialism becoming a directly economic relationship, even if that relationship requires brutal force to implant and sustain it. That kind of relationship could be justified, or so it appeared, not by the right to rule, nor even just the right to appropriate unoccupied or unused land, but by the right, indeed the obligation, to produce exchange-value.

Before the economic hegemony of capital came to dominate the world, capitalism passed through the classic age of imperialism, with all its intense geopolitical and military rivalries. That age is now long over. Capitalist imperialism has become almost entirely a matter of economic domination, in which market imperatives, manipulated by the dominant capitalist powers, are made to do the work no longer done by imperial states or colonial settlers. But we are now discovering that the universality of capitalist imperatives has not at all removed the need for military force. If anything, the contrary is true. The new imperialism cannot dispense, as did Locke's theory of colonial expropriation, with a doctrine of war.

It is, again, a distinctive and essential characteristic of capitalist imperialism that its economic reach far exceeds its direct political and military grasp. It can rely on the economic imperatives of 'the market' to do much of its imperial work. This sharply differentiates it from earlier forms of imperialism, which depended directly on such extra-economic powers – whether territorial empires which could reach only as far as the capacity of their direct coercive powers to impose their rule, or commercial empires whose advantages depended on domination of the seas or other trade routes.

The imposition of economic imperatives can be a very bloody business. But once subordinate powers are made vulnerable to those imperatives and the 'laws' of the market, direct rule by imperial states is no longer required to impose the will of capital. Yet here, again, we encounter the paradox that, while market imperatives may reach far beyond the power of any single state, these imperatives themselves must be enforced by extra-economic power. Neither the imposition of economic imperatives nor the everyday social order demanded by capital accumulation and the operations of the market can be achieved without the help of administrative and coercive powers much more local and territorially limited than the economic reach of capital.

That is why, paradoxically, the more purely *economic* empire has become, the more the nation state has proliferated. Not only imperial powers but subordinate states have proved necessary to the rule of global capital. It has even, as we have seen, been a major strategy of capitalist imperialism to create local states to act as conduits for capitalist imperatives. Nor has globalization transcended this imperial need for a system of states. The 'globalized' world is more than ever a world of nation states. The new imperialism we call globalization, precisely because it depends on a wide-ranging economic hegemony that reaches far beyond any state's territorial boundaries or political domination, is a form of imperialism more dependent than any other on a system of multiple states.

Surplus Imperialism?

We are told that war without boundaries is a response to a world without borders, a world in which nation states are no longer the principal players and non-state adversaries, or 'terrorists', have become a major threat. That argument has a certain appealing symmetry, but it will not stand up to scrutiny. The danger of terrorism, more than any other threat of force, is resistant to overwhelming military opposition – not despite but because of its statelessness; and, in any case, the 'war against terrorism' is likely to promote more terrorist attacks than it prevents. The menace of non-state enemies cannot explain the disproportionate concentration of military force, directed at no identifiable objective. On the contrary, 'surplus imperialism' makes sense, however perverted and even ultimately self-defeating, only as a response to the global state system and its contradictory dynamics.

Global capital needs local states. But, while states acting at the behest of global capital may be more effective than the old colonial settlers who once carried capitalist imperatives throughout the world, they also pose great risks. In particular, they are subject to their own internal pressures and oppositional forces; and their own coercive powers can fall into the wrong hands, which may oppose the will of imperial capital. In this globalized world where the nation state is supposed to be dying, the irony is that, because the new imperialism depends more than ever on a system of multiple states to maintain global order, it matters more than ever what local forces govern them and how.

One significant if not immediate danger is that popular struggles for truly democratic states, for a transformation in the balance of class forces in the state, with international solidarity among such democratic national struggles, might present a greater challenge to imperial power than ever before. In a world in which disparities between rich and poor are not diminishing but growing, this possibility, however remote it may seem, can never be far from the imperial consciousness. Nor is the imperial hegemon oblivious to the growing disaffection and anti-systemic sentiment generated by neo-liberal globalization all over the world, North and South.[7] US-led global capital cannot welcome even the kind of electoral change that, as this book was being completed, was occurring in Brazil.

But with or without an immediate threat of widespread 'regime change' in the wrong direction, the US has worked very hard to maintain a political environment within which US 'global' capital can move freely. The imperial power has therefore regularly acted to insure against any risk of losing its hold on the global state system. However unlikely or distant that prospect may seem, the US has been ready to anticipate it by flaunting its one most unambiguous advantage, its overwhelming military power – if only because it can do so more or less with impunity.

There are several quite distinct dangers that may threaten this US-dominated global system, which all have to do with the state. One is the disorder engendered by the *absence* of effective state powers – such as today's so-called 'failed' states – which endanger the stable and predictable environment that capital needs. Another is the threat from states operating outside the normal scope of the US-dominated world order, what Washington likes to call 'rogue' states (or 'the axis of evil') – which are distinguished from equally evil states that do remain within the US orbit.

Yet an even greater challenge is posed not by such marginal cases but by states and economies that may function all too well and threaten to contest US supremacy. Such threats come not only from possible future competitors like China or Russia. There are more immediate challenges within the capitalist order and even at its very core. The European Union, for instance, is potentially a stronger economic power than the US.

But maintaining hegemony among major capitalist powers is a far more complicated business than achieving geopolitical dominance, or even a 'balance of power', as old imperial states sought to do in the days of traditional interimperialist rivalry. It is no longer a simple matter of defeating rivals. War with major capitalist competitors, while it can never be ruled out, is likely to be self-defeating, destroying not only competition but markets and investment opportunities at the same time. Imperial dominance in a global capitalist economy requires a delicate and contradictory balance between suppressing competition and maintaining conditions in competing economies that generate markets and profit. This is one of the most fundamental contradictions of the new world order.

The contradictory relations among major capitalist states are nicely illustrated by the development of Germany and Japan after World War II, and their relationship with former adversaries. Their economic success was, from the US point of view, inseparably both good and bad, supplying markets and capital, but also competitive threats. Relations among the major capitalist nations have been maintained in an uneasy balance between competition and cooperation ever since, with major disagreements regularly erupting, but without a threat of war.

Imperial hegemony in the world of global capitalism, then, means controlling rival economies and states without going to war with them. At the same time, the new military doctrine is based on the assumption that military power is an indispensable tool in maintaining the critical balance, even if its application in controlling major competitors must be indirect. This is especially true when other economies are rising in relation to the hegemonic power. It has certainly not escaped the notice of the 'only superpower' that, while its own economy was (and still is?) in decline, some other parts of the world, notably China, were experiencing historically unprecedented growth.[8] The emergence of the European Union as an economic superpower has also placed a special premium on military supremacy as the only reliable index of US hegemony.

'The Europeans are learning', writes a former Foreign Editor of *Newsweek* in the authoritative journal, *Foreign Affairs*, 'what the Japanese learned in the Persian Gulf War: vast economic power gives you leverage mainly in economics. . . . Tokyo proved during the Gulf War that it was not ready, it turned out, to be the new Rome of the "Pacific Century". And in this now-critical realm of hard power, Europe has, like Japan, been shown to be a "pygmy". . . .'[9] This assessment occurs in a critique of US unilateralism, written in the hope that Europe will rise to the challenge. But the current US military doctrine of uncontestable (and very expensive) supremacy is clearly designed to discourage any substantial build-up of independent Japanese and European military forces – not only because this ensures US predominance in the 'realm of hard power' but precisely because 'hard power' has its own effects on economic 'leverage'.

The US is prepared to encourage the development of European military forces up to a point, if their nature and use can be confined to serving its purposes – for instance, European peace-keeping forces can play a useful role in cleaning up the mess left by US military action, or specialized forces of various kinds can be deployed in the 'war on terror'. But every care is being taken to prevent the emergence of any truly independent military rival in Europe. The preferred strategy is to keep European forces safely within the embrace of NATO, where they can be (as the shrewd US commentator, William Pfaff has described it) the 'foreign legion of the Pentagon'. 'A modernized European NATO force offers added value to Washington in two respects', writes Pfaff:

> First, it would preempt resources and energies that could otherwise go into the European Union's independent rapid reaction force. Second, its modernized weapons systems and structures would be integrated into American command, control and communications systems, with the effect that they would function in degraded mode outside US/NATO operations. These are not unimportant considerations in the eyes of some hawkish Wash-

ington policy thinkers who consider Europe the only possible
future challenger to US global predominance other than China.[10]

To put it another way, the principal function of NATO, now more
than ever, has less to do with forging an alliance against common
enemies than maintaining US hegemony over its friends. A military
doctrine, then, has been evolving in the US to deal with the
contradictions of global capitalism. Its first premise is that the US
must have such a degree of military supremacy that no other state or
combination of states, friend or foe, will be tempted to contest or
equal it. The purpose of this strategy is not simply to deter attack
but above all to ensure that no other state will aspire to global or
even regional dominance.

The Bush Doctrine

In 1992, the *New York Times* published a leaked document, *Defense
Planning Guidance*, produced by the Pentagon. The author was Paul
Wolfowitz, who wrote it for the benefit of George Bush Senior and
is now advising George W., while its principal supporter when it first
appeared was Dick Cheney, the current Vice-President. The logic of
this document is fairly convoluted, but its meaning is nonetheless
clear: the object of maintaining the US military posture, in the
Middle East as elsewhere, has less to do with, for instance, protecting
the US oil supply, than with discouraging 'advanced industrial
nations from challenging our leadership'. Aspiring powers in Asia
and Europe in particular must be confronted with a military dominance capable of 'deterring potential competitors from even aspiring
to a larger regional or global role.'[11] The goal is what has been called
'full spectrum dominance', extending even into space.

This document clearly demonstrates that the 'total' war advocated by Richard Perle is not just a response to '9/11'. If anything, that tragic event has been used as a pretext for activating a long-standing agenda. Even the less rabidly hawkish Colin Powell subscribes to the goal of, as one commentator puts it, 'unilateral world domination', insisting already in 1992 that the US must have sufficient power 'to deter any challenger from ever dreaming of challenging us on the world stage'.[12]

The doctrine outlined in *Defense Planning Guidance* has now been given official status in George W. Bush's new *National Security Strategy*, issued in September 2002. The Bush doctrine calls for a unilateral and exclusive right to preemptive attack, any time, anywhere, unfettered by any international agreements, to ensure that '[o]ur forces will be strong enough to dissuade potential adversaries from pursuing a military build-up in hope of surpassing, or equalling, the power of the United States.'

Ever since it was first enunciated, the object of this doctrine has not escaped various commentators, whether sympathetic or critical. It has been clear to them that the targets of military strategy may not always be the obvious ones and that hegemony over major competitors, including friends and allies, has been an overriding objective. 'We do not get that large a percentage of oil from the Middle East . . .', writes one analyst, '[a]nd one of the reasons that we are sort of assuming this role of policeman of the Middle East has more to do with making Japan and some other countries feel that their oil flow is assured . . . so that they don't then feel more need to create a great power, armed forces, and security doctrine, and you don't start getting a lot of great powers with conflicting interests sending their military powers all over the world.' This observation may underestimate the importance to the US of Middle East oil, but it is surely not wrong about the US interest in discouraging the military independence of friendly competitors. Two other commentators have even suggested that the resolution of certain world conflicts is not in US interests because it undermines the justification for a military force larger and more powerful than all its competitors combined. 'The best situation', for instance, 'is the status quo in Korea, which allows US forces to be stationed there indefinitely', while Korean reunification would be likely to encourage Japan to become militarily self-sufficient, as US troops pulled out.[13]

It has become a convention among critics of the Bush administration that this strategy represents a major break with earlier US foreign policy. For decades after World War II, it is argued, that policy was grounded in 'realism', which called for containment of the Soviet Union, and a kind of 'liberalism', in which '[o]pen trade, democracy, and multilateral institutional relations went together'.[14] Yet, without the continuities between then and now, the Bush administration's reckless adventurism would be completely inexplicable. We cannot, of course, discount the idiosyncratic irrationalities or the extremist politics of the personalities surrounding Bush, or, indeed, their very particular and personal interests in the oil industry. But the foundations of the current strategy were laid long ago.

There can be no doubt that Bush's contempt for international agreements has taken US unilateralism to new extremes. Yet there is nothing new in the Bush team's conviction that the principal objective of US foreign policy is to establish hegemony over a global system of more or less sovereign states, and that massive military superiority lies at the core of that project. The legendary Cold War Secretary of State, John Foster Dulles, was already very clear about this in the 1950s; and, while the new doctrine of preemptive attack is, not unreasonably, regarded as a break with earlier doctrines of deterrence, there was no great distance to travel from Dulles's 'massive [i.e. disproportionate] retaliation' to Bush's 'preemptive retaliation'.

What has changed is not the underlying principles of US military doctrine so much as the conditions in which they must operate. In the postwar period, the US was virtually unchallenged as an economic power. While the long boom was accompanied by a growing military supremacy, the US, despite the Soviet challenge, could more or less safely rely on its economic dominance to manage the capitalist world – though even then, enveloping potential rivals in US-dominated military alliances was essential to its hegemonic strategy. Today, US economic dominance is no longer so unchallenged. At the same time, its military supremacy is now so massive and forbidding that friendly rivals have no incentive to incur the costs of matching it. In that combination of circumstances, it is hardly surprising that the US is increasingly turning to military force to consolidate its hegemony and the economic advantages that come with it – for instance, through control of oil.

Nor have ostensibly more benign administrations, like that of Bill Clinton, departed significantly from this military doctrine. They have, if anything, pushed the boundaries of war even further, with their notion of 'humanitarian' war, which is not a million miles away from Dulles's contention that mere 'deterrence' should be replaced by active 'liberation', in a foreign policy with 'heart'. It is unlikely that Clinton would have pushed this strategy to the extremity of the Bush Doctrine, and he might have avoided an ultimately self-defeating engagement in the most reckless military adventures to which the Bush administration seems attracted. But if there has been a break between previous postwar administrations and the current Bush regime, it is certainly not in the underlying principles of US global hegemony and military supremacy.

Today's Bush Doctrine is, to be sure, a distinctively extreme manifestation of the old strategic vision. But, as self-defeating as it is likely to be, it has its roots in the vast imperial ambitions that have guided US foreign policy since World War II. It is not hard to see how a project of global economic hegemony, coupled with a dangerous mode of imperial administration through the medium of multiple states, might move inexorably in the direction now taken by Bush. It was probably only a matter of time before the whole world, and not just a Communist enemy, would come to be regarded as a potential adversary, requiring a military dominance to match the threat. That the current military stance is counterproductive, inevitably generating growing anti-imperial hostility throughout the world, certainly represents a contradiction in the new imperialism. But both sides of that contradiction belong to the essential logic of this imperial system.

The disappearance of the other major superpower with the collapse of the Soviet Union has, needless to say, profoundly changed the global order. If nothing else, it has removed the last remaining reality check on US global ambitions. It could, of course, be argued that the removal of its principal adversary should have moderated the US compulsion to achieve ever more massive global supremacy, and that it is hard to understand where the motivation now comes from, when the US is already so clearly supreme. But, if anything, the absence of the Soviet Union has complicated the maintenance of US hegemony over its allies. In any case, hyper-dominance creates a logic and momentum of its own. Unilateral global supremacy can never be achieved once and for all. It means moving the boundaries of warfare ever further beyond the reach of would-be challengers; and this requires constant revolutionizing of the means of war – which cannot then be left untested and unused.

Who Will Guard the Guardians?

The deployment of US military force does not, then, have simple and direct objectives. It plays a complex role in sustaining a system of compliant states, and with it come new ideological requirements. The old forms of colonial imperialism required outright conquest of subject peoples and military defeat of recalcitrant rivals, together with appropriate theories of war and peace. Early capitalist imperialism, while no less dependent on coercive force to take control of colonial territory, seemed able to dispense with a political defence of colonization and to incorporate the justification of colonial settlement into a theory of property. Globalization, the economic imperialism of capital taken to its logical conclusion, has, paradoxically, required a new doctrine of extra-economic, and especially military, coercion.

The practical and doctrinal difficulties posed by the new situation are obvious. If local states will guard the economy, who will guard the guardians? It could, perhaps, be argued that US economic dominance is powerful enough to win compliance from any conceivable opponent, without the threat of war. But, even if we set aside the economic challenge of the major competitors, the system of multiple states is unpredictable, and military power is the ultimate insurance. If the object is indeed 'unilateral world domination' in this global state system, nothing less than absolute military superiority will be enough to ensure that the will of the hegemon will never be thwarted. Although the constant threat of force against all comers may in the end be self-defeating, the hegemon, once embarked on global economic domination in a world of multiple states, could hardly contemplate proceeding without a commensurately dominant military power.

Yet it is not easy to specify the role of military force in establishing and defending imperial control over a global economy, instead of sovereignty over a clearly bounded territory. It is impossible for any single state power, even the massive military force of the US, to impose itself every day, everywhere, throughout the global system. No conceivable force can impose the will of global capital all the time on a multitude of subordinate states, or maintain the predictable order required by capital's daily transactions. For that matter, military force is a very blunt instrument and completely unsuited to supply the daily legal and political conditions for capital accumulation. So military power may have to be mobilized less to achieve specific objectives, against specific targets and adversaries, than simply to make its presence known and to assert its uncontestable supremacy.

In any case, since even US military power cannot be active everywhere at once (it has never even aspired to more than two local wars at a time), the only option is to demonstrate, by frequent displays of military force, that it can go anywhere at any time, and do great damage. This is not to say that war will be constant – which would be too disruptive to the economic order. 'Operation Infinite War' is apparently intended to produce something more like Hobbes's 'state of war': 'the nature of war', he writes in the *Leviathan*, 'consisteth not in actual fighting, but in the known disposition thereto during all the time there is no assurance to the contrary'. It is this endless *possibility* of war that imperial capital needs to sustain its hegemony over the global system of multiple states.

Nor does this necessarily mean that the US will wage war for no reason at all, just for the purpose of display. Control of oil supplies is now, as before, a major motivation in imperial ventures. The attack on Afghanistan was undertaken with an eye to the huge oil and gas reserves of Central Asia. Although Afghanistan itself is evidently of no consequence to the US, which seems prepared to forego 'nation-building' there and to let the country relapse into self-destructive chaos, the war has had the advantage of strengthening the US military presence in the region. The grab for oil in Iraq, to benefit US oil companies at the expense of competitors, and to consolidate global hegemony through control of oil, is a rather more difficult case. Sitting on its own huge oil reserves, and with a well developed political and economic infrastructure, to say nothing of its military forces, Iraq cannot, like Afghanistan, be left to its own devices. We now know that the Bush administration's preferred option is outright occupation by the US, under military rule and with direct control of Iraqi oil – at least until that control has passed largely into the hands of US-dominated oil companies.[15]

Yet whatever specific objectives US wars may have, there is always something more. There is, of course, the long-established need to sustain the 'military–industrial complex', which has been so central to the US economy. Just as the Cold War did in its time, the new endless war is vital to an economy so dependent on military production, on the militarization of the aerospace industry and on the global arms trade. An endless state of war can serve many other domestic purposes too – as the Cold War also did. The climate of fear deliberately fostered by the Bush administration is being used not only to justify military programmes and the erosion of civil liberties, but a far more wide-ranging domestic agenda, which seemed unattainable before September 11. Even the threat of war in Iraq was timed to influence Congressional elections. There is nothing like a state of war to consolidate domestic rule, especially in the US.

But, again, the larger purpose of the perpetual state of war goes beyond all this: to shape the political environment in a global system of multiple states. This complex system, which includes not just 'evil' states with 'weapons of mass destruction' but also friendly competitors and exploitable economies, requires a complex strategy and a variety of military functions.

In some cases, the object of military force is indeed exemplary terror, *pour encourager les autres*, or what has been called the 'demonstration effect'. This was, according to right-wing US commentators like Charles Krauthammer, the main purpose of the war in Afghanistan, designed to spread fear throughout the region and beyond. In other cases, there may be direct intervention to bring about 'regime change'. In the Middle East, we are already seeing something like a return to an earlier imperialism, with the fairly explicit intention of restructuring the region even more directly in the interests of US capital. The new imperialism may here be coming full circle. Like the British in India, when commercial imperialism gave way to direct imperial rule, the US may be finding that empire creates its own territorial imperative.

In yet other cases, especially in the advanced capitalist states, the political environment is shaped indirectly. Just as the state of war is intended to create the right political climate at home in the US, allies are drawn into its hegemonic orbit by their implication in pacts and alliances and by means of a military supremacy so daunting and expensive that other major economic powers will see no point in seeking to match it.[16] In all cases, the overriding objective is to demonstrate and consolidate US domination over the system of multiples states.

Such purposes help to explain why the US wields such disproportionate military power, why there has developed a pattern of resort to military action by the US in situations ill-suited to military solutions, why massive military action is anything but a last resort, and why the connection between means and ends in these military ventures is typically so tenuous.

This war without end in purpose or time belongs to an endless empire without boundaries or even territory. Yet this is an empire that must be administered by institutions and powers which do indeed have territorial boundaries. The consequence of a globalized economy has been that capital depends more, not less, on a system of local states to manage the economy, and states have become more, not less, involved in organizing economic circuits. This means that the old capitalist division of labour between capital and state, between economic and political power, has been disrupted. At the same time, there is a growing gulf between the global economic reach of capital and the local powers it needs to sustain it, and the military doctrine of the Bush regime is an attempt to fill the gap.

In its efforts to resolve these contradictions, the Bush Doctrine certainly represents a danger to the whole world, but it also testifies to the risks and instabilities of a global empire that relies on many local states, a global economy managed by local administrations and national states which are vulnerable to challenge by truly democratic struggles. In the disparity between global economic power and its local political supports, there is surely an expanding space for opposition.

NOTES

PREFACE TO THE PAPERBACK EDITION

1. One reference, right at the beginning of the book, appeared in a footnote which, I regret to say, went missing in the Verso publication process, although it had appeared in the earlier, Indian edition published by LeftWord, as the first footnote in the Introduction. The correction has been made for this paperback edition.
2. For a critique of *Empire*, see my essay 'A Manifesto for Global Capitalism?' in the collection *Debating Empire*, edited by Gopal Balakrishnan (London and New York: Verso, 2003).

INTRODUCTION

1. Not long after these words were written newspapers reported plans by the US to occupy Iraq after going to war.
2. To put it briefly, Marx explains that workers are paid for their labour *power*, not for the fruits of their labour. The capitalist pays a wage to buy that labour power, typically for a fixed period of time, and thereby gains

control of everything the worker produces during that time, which can then be sold on the market. The object, then, is to maximize the difference between what capital pays for labour power and what it can derive from the products of labour.

3. Philip Bobbitt, *The Shield of Achilles* (London: Allen Lane Penguin, 2002); Michael Hardt and Antonio Negri, *Empire* (Cambridge, Mass.: Harvard University Press, 2000). Given *Empire*'s central premise and its implications for resistance, it is perhaps not surprising that this book received such respectful attention in unexpected quarters in the mainstream, far from anti-capitalist or anti-globalization, press. This argument is developed at length in my 'A Manifesto for Global Capital?' in G. Balakrishnan, ed., *Debating Empire* (London and New York: Verso, 2003).

1   THE DETACHMENT OF ECONOMIC POWER

1. This chapter is based on my article, 'Where is the Power of Capital: Globalization and the Nation State', in Alfredo Saad-Filho, ed., *Anti-Capitalism: A Marxist Introduction* (London: Pluto Press, 2002).

2. Gerard Greenfield, 'Devastating, with a Difference: From Anti-Corporate Populism to Anti-Capitalist Alternatives', *Against the Current* 93, July/August 2001, pp. 12–14. The quotations are from pp. 13 and 14.

2   THE EMPIRE OF PROPERTY

1. Keith Hopkins, *Conquerors and Slaves*, (Cambridge: Cambridge University Press, 1978), pp. 14 and 30.

2. Feudal property was, in principle, 'owned' by king or church and only 'held' by landlords and tenants. But this did not prevent – on the contrary, feudalism promoted – the emergence of powerful landed classes, whose wealth and power were rooted in the possession of land. It may be misleading, in strictly legal terms, to describe feudal property as 'private', but there is no other simple way of distinguishing between this form of property and state appropriation through the medium of office – a distinction expressed in the differentiation of 'private' rent and 'public' tax. Even post-feudal conquerors and colonists in the Spanish

colonies, for instance, were given land grants or rights of usufruct in land legally 'owned' by Spanish monarchs; but there is no mistaking the difference between this class of 'private' landholders and, say, a prosperous Chinese mandarin enriched by state office but restricted in his possession of land.

3. On the Latin American peoples encountered by the conquerors, see Mark A. Burkholder and Lyman L. Johnson, *Colonial Latin America* (Oxford: Oxford University press, 4th ed., 2001).

4. For an illuminating discussion of Spanish imperialist ideology, in contrast to British and French, see Anthony Pagden, *Lords of All the World: Ideologies of Empire in Spain, Britain and France c. 1500–1800* (New Haven and London: Yale University Press, 1995).

3   THE EMPIRE OF COMMERCE

1. Albert Hourani, *A History of the Arab Peoples* (London: Faber and Faber, 1991), p. 130.

2. On this point, see Justin Rosenberg, *The Empire of Civil Society* (London: Verso, 1993).

3. John Hale, *The Civilization of Europe in the Renaissance* (New York: Simon and Schuster, 1993), p. 150.

4. I discuss the Dutch economy at greater length in 'The Question of Market Dependence', *Journal of Agrarian Change*, Vol. 2 No. 1, January 2002, pp. 50–87. The discussion relies heavily on the evidence provided by Jan de Vries and Ad van der Woude in *The first modern economy: success, failure, and perseverance of the Dutch economy, 1500–1815* (Cambridge: Cambridge University Press, 1997), though I come to rather different conclusions about its non-capitalist character. My article in *JAC* engages in a discussion with Robert Brenner's earlier article in the same journal, 'The Low Countries in the Transition to Capitalism', *JAC*, Vol. 1 No. 2, April 2001, pp. 169–241, which regards the Dutch economy as capitalist.

5. See Joyce Mastboom, 'On Their Own Terms: Peasant Households' Response to Capitalist Development', *History of Political Thought* XXI.3, Autumn 2000, and 'Protoindustrialization and Agriculture in the Eastern Netherlands', *Social Science History*, 20(2), pp. 235–258.

6. Jan de Vries and Ad van der Woude, *The first modern economy*, p. 502.

7. Ibid., p. 596.

8. On the scale of early Dutch taxation and its uses, see ibid., especially pp. 100 and 111.

9. This section is based on my article, 'Infinite War', *Historical Materialism*, Vol. 10 No. 1, 2002.

10. For a provocative, and persuasive, interpretation of Grotius, see Richard Tuck, *The Rights of War and Peace: Political Thought and the International Order from Grotius to Kant* (Oxford: Oxford University Press, 1999).

11. Richard Tuck, *The Rights of War and Peace*, p. 85.

12. Ibid., p. 108.

13. Anthony Pagden has a useful discussion of this principle and its use particularly by the English and, to a lesser degree, the French, and the reasons for its absence in Spanish imperial ideology. See *Lords of All the World*, pp. 77 *passim*. The principle was obviously more useful in cases where imperialism took the form of settler colonies which displaced local populations and was of little use to the Spanish, with their empire of explicit conquest over often densely populated and cultivated territories.

4   A NEW KIND OF EMPIRE

1. R.H. Tawney, *The Agrarian Problem in the Sixteenth Century* (London: Longmans, Green and Co., 1912), p. 189.

2. 'Laboratories of empire' is the phrase used by Jane Ohlmeyer, ' "Civilizinge of those rude partes": Colonization within Britain and Ireland, 1580s-1640s', in Nicholas Canny, ed., *The Origins of Empire* (Oxford: Oxford University Press, 1998), p. 146. On the process of subduing and 'unifying' the British Isles, see Steven G. Ellis and Sarah Barber, eds, *Conquest and Union: Fashioning a British State: 1485–1725* (London and New York: Longman, 1995).

3. Nicholas Canny, 'The Origins of Empire: An Introduction', in *Origins of Empire*, p. 15.

4. Steven Ellis, *Ireland in the age of the Tudors, 1447–1603: English expansion and the end of Gaelic rule* (London and New York: Longman, 1998), p. 15.

5. Ohlmeyer, p. 127.

6. R.F. Foster, ed., *The Oxford History of Ireland* (Oxford: Oxford University Press, 1992), pp. 122–3.
7. Charles Webster, *The Great Instauration: science, medicine and reform, 1626–1660* (London: Duckworth, 1975), p. 453.
8. Ibid., p. 455.
9. Quoted in ibid., p. 456.

5 THE OVERSEAS EXPANSION OF ECONOMIC IMPERATIVES

1. Anthony Pagden, *Lords of All the World: Ideologies of Empire in Spain, Britain and France c.1500–1800* (New Haven and London: Yale University Press, 1995), p. 93
2. Ibid., p. 73
3. Ibid., p. 78
4. Quoted in ibid., pp. 78–9.
5. Richard Tuck, *The Rights of War and Peace: Politcal Thought and the International Order from Grotius to Kant* (Oxford: Oxford University Press, 1999), pp. 191–96.
6. James Tully, whose work has revealed much about the imperialist implications of Locke's theory of property, suggests that, in Locke's view, Amerindian society lacked any legitimate civil government, and property was something less than full property, remaining the kind of possession that exists in the state of nature. See Tully, *An Approach to Political Philosophy: Locke in Contexts* (Cambridge: Cambridge University Press, 1993), pp. 138–9. To be sure, Tully's argument emphasizes the importance of the distinction between 'waste' and improvement as the basis of property rights. But the implication here seems to be that Locke's views of property and civil government in Amerindian society are distinct but related, since it is the absence of a true civil government that leaves Indians in something like a state of nature, in which property cannot be complete. If this were really Locke's argument, it might help to account for the absence, in his theory, of any need for consent by local authorities in the expropriation of Indian land. But the contention that Locke denies the presence of proper civil government in Amerindian society is itself

open to question, and, more importantly, there is no connection between the presence or absence of civil government and the quality of Indian property. It is, in fact, remarkable that Locke scarcely raises the question of legitimate government in his account of property, and certainly does not argue that Amerindians lack real property because they lack civil society. They lack true property because there is no proper money, commerce, and improvement for commercial profit. In other words, the point is not that he waives the need for consent by a civil authority on the grounds that there is no such civil authority, but rather that he by-passes the question of political jurisdiction altogether because the right of appropriation rests on a different foundation.

7. David Richardson, 'The British Empire and the Atlantic Slave Trade, 1660–1807', *The Oxford History of the British Empire: The Eighteenth Century* (Oxford: Oxford University Press, 1998), p. 440.

8. Notably, Eric Williams in *Capitalism and Slavery*, published in 1944.

9. See, for instance, David Richardson, 'The British Empire and the Atlantic Slave Trade', p. 461.

10. Charles Post, 'The Agrarian Origins of US Capitalism: The Transformation of the Northern Countryside Before the Civil War', *Journal of Peasant Studies*, Vol. 22 no. 3, April 1995, pp. 416–17.

11. D.A. Washbrook, 'India, 1818–1860: The Two Faces of Colonialism', in Andrew Porter ed., *The Oxford History of the British Empire: The Nineteenth Century* (Oxford: Oxford University Press, 1999), pp 398–99. On the deindustrialization and deurbanization of India, see C.A. Bayly, *Indian Society and the Making of the British Empire* (Cambridge: Cambridge University Press, 1989), chap. 5.

12. Patrick K. O'Brien, 'The Costs and Benefits of British Imperialism 1846–1914', *Past and Present* 120, August 1988, p. 199.

6   THE INTERNATIONALIZATION OF CAPITALIST IMPERATIVES

1. Paul Kennedy, *The Rise and Fall of the Great Powers: Economic Change and Military Conflict from 1500–2000* (London: Fontana Press, 1989), p. 171.

2. Rosa Luxemburg, *The Accumulation of Capital* (London: Routledge and Kegan Paul, 1963), p. 467.

3. Jonathan Steele, 'East Timor is independent. So long as it does as it's told', the *Guardian*, 23 May, 2002.

4. On the long downturn, see Robert Brenner, *The Economics of Global Turbulence: Uneven Development and the Long Downturn, The Advanced Capitalist Economies from Boom to Stagnation*, special issue of *New Left Review*, no. 229 (May–June 1998). On displacing capitalist crisis in space and time, see David Harvey, *The Limits to Capital* (London: Verso, 1999). On the displacement of overaccumulated capital and its effects on Africa, see Patrick Bond, *Against Global Apartheid: South Africa Meets the World Bank, IMF and International Finance* (Cape Town: University of Cape Town Press, 2001, especially pp. 7–10.

5. These are the findings of an Economic and Social Research Council study, as summarized by Professor Alan Rugman, quoted in Larry Elliott, 'Big business isn't really that big', the *Guardian*, 2 September, 2002, p. 23.

7 'SURPLUS IMPERIALISM', WAR WITHOUT END

1. Paul Kennedy, 'The Eagle Has Landed', *Financial Times Weekend*, February 2–3, 2002, p. I.

2. I owe this phrase to Robert Brenner.

3. This section is based on my article, 'Infinite War', in *Historical Materialism*, Vol. 10 No. 1, 2002.

4. Ed Vulliamy, 'Inside the Pentagon', the *Observer*, 30 September, 2001.

5. An interesting symptom of the latter tendency is a scurrilous document entitled 'Defending Civilization: How Our Universities Are Failing America', which denounces academic critics of the so-called 'war on terrorism' as traitors. The document, produced by the American Council of Trustees and Alumni, an organization co-founded by Lynne Cheney, the US Vice-President's wife, named names, in a manner reminiscent of the infamous McCarthy era. Mrs. Cheney is also the author of a children's book, *America: A Patriotic Primer*, an A to Z of jingoistic propaganda.

6. Richard Perle, quoted in John Pilger, *The New Rulers of the World* (London: Verso, 2002), pp. 9–10.

7. For an excellent brief discussion of the current 'legitimacy crisis', see Walden Bello, 'Drop Till We Shop?', a review of Robert Brenner's *The Boom and the Bubble: The US in the World Economy*, in *The Nation*, 21 October, 2002, especially pp. 27–29.

8. On the contrasts between the long economic downturn in the West, especially in the US, and remarkable rises elsewhere at the same time – with China, for instance, experiencing growth rates during the West's long downturn that 'dwarfed' even those of the postwar boom in the West – see Perry Anderson, 'Confronting Defeat', an essay on Eric Hobsbawm's history of the contemporary world, in *London Review of Books*, 17 October, 2002, p. 12.

9. Michael Hirsh, 'Bush and the World', *Foreign Affairs*, September/October 2002, p. 38

10. William Pfaff, 'A foreign legion for the Pentagon? NATO's "relevance"', *International Herald Tribune*, Thursday 7 November, 2002, p. 8.

11. Quoted in Nick Cohen, 'With a friend like this . . .', the *Observer*, 7 April, 2002, p. 29.

12. Quoted in Anatol Lieven, 'The Push for War', *London Review of Books*, 3 October, 2002, p. 8.

13. Walter Russell Mead, from the Council on Foreign Relations; and Christopher Layne and Benjamin Schwartz, in the *Atlantic Monthly*, both quoted by Nick Cohen. Cohen also points out that US oil comes largely from other regions – Canada, Mexico, Venezuela and producers at home, with Russia promising to become a major source – while only a quarter comes from the Persian Gulf.

14. G. John Ikenberry, 'America's Imperial Ambition', *Foreign Affairs*, September/October 2002, p. 47.

15. Plans for US occupation of Iraq came to light as this book was going to press.

16. On US strategies of domination, see Peter Gowan, *The Global Gamble: Washington's Faustian Bid for World Domination* (London: Verso, 1999). See also Gowan's Deutscher Memorial Lecture, 'American Global Government: Will it Work?', forthcoming in *Socialist Register*. Gowan stresses US concerns about the challenge posed by Western European powers, notably Germany.

INDEX